Pie

pie [pahy], noun

· ·

100 essential recipes

Pie

pie [pahy], noun

···

100 essential recipes

spruce

An Hachette UK Company
www.hachette.co.uk

First published in Great Britain in 2014 by Spruce
A division of Octopus Publishing Group Ltd
Endeavour House, 189 Shaftesbury Avenue, London, WC2H 8JY
www.octopusbooks.co.uk
www.octopusbooksusa.com

Distributed in the US by Hachette Book Group USA
237 Park Avenue, New York, NY 10017, USA

Distributed in Canada by Canadian Manda Group
165 Dufferin Street, Toronto, Ontario, Canada M6K 3H6

ISBN 978 1 84601 431 4

Printed and bound in China

10 9 8 7 6 5 4 3 2 1

CONSULTANT PUBLISHER Sarah Ford
EDITOR Jo Wilson
COPY-EDITOR Jo Richardson
DESIGNER Eoghan O'Brien & Clare Barber
ILLUSTRATOR Abigail Read
PRODUCTION CONTROLLER Sarah Connelly

CONTENTS

INTRODUCTION

Pies are the ultimate comfort food. They are hearty and warming, and show off homemade baking at its best. Whether you are settling down for a family meal or preparing a sweet pie to share with friends, the care and attention that go into the preparation of a pie ensure even the most humble ingredients are transformed into something truly special.

Pies are often the meal of choice for celebrations, social events, and family gatherings—think of Thanksgiving and you immediately think of pie. The very essence of the pie means it is designed for sharing; people gather round the table to eat together and are served from one dish. However, this hearty meal doesn't have ideas above its station—it is equally at home on the midweek dinner table as it is at a festive get-together. In fact, it is the versatility of the pie that makes it so valued. Ever since the Pilgrims landed in America, pies have been prepared for every occasion and from every imaginable ingredient—from leftovers to rare breed meat. But whatever the flavor, it is the sentiment that gives the pie such a prominent place in our culinary history.

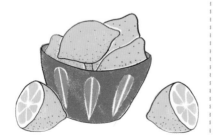

ESSENTIAL EQUIPMENT

If you are planning to make a lot of pies, it's definitely worth investing in a few key pieces of good-quality equipment. If you spend a little more initially, you will be rewarded with years of use, so it is money well spent.

MIXING BOWLS

Choose a selection of sizes and make sure you have at least one bowl that's ceramic or metal (plastic bowls should not be used for whipping egg whites).

MEASURING SPOONS AND CUPS

Good measuring equipment is essential for pastry work, as the ingredients need to be measured carefully. A variety of sizes of measuring cups will ensure you are prepared for all types of recipe and a good set of cups will last for many years.

ROLLING PINS

Although wooden rolling pins are often the default choice, pastry can be temperamental and it makes sense to keep a ceramic rolling pin in the drawer for any sticky situations.

PIE DISHES

These are also called pie pans or pie plates and there is a huge variety of makes, materials, and sizes to choose from. A pie dish has sloped sides and may sometimes have a fluted edge for decorative crusts. Many people favor Pyrex pie pans but it really comes down to personal preference—the different materials don't have a great impact on the baking of the pie. The only other factor to consider is whether you want a pan with a removable bottom. Again, this is down to the individual and is really only a consideration if you are planning to remove your pies from the pan in order to show off the pie crust.

WIRE RACK

Although a lot of pies are eaten warm, you need to let others cool, so wire racks should be on your equipment list.

KEY INGREDIENTS

The following are the essential pantry ingredients needed for making most pie recipes:

- **All-purpose flour**
- **Fat**—this could be butter or shortening (vegetable or otherwise)
- **Seasoning**—salt is needed for pastry, and salt and pepper are both essential for seasoning savory pie fillings

Some recipes also require eggs (make sure these are really fresh), sugar (keep a stock of superfine and brown sugar), and milk.

If you also have ingredients like stock, ground spices, dried fruits and nuts, citrus fruits, unsweetened cocoa, and vanilla extract tucked away in your cabinets, you will be able to create even more recipes at a moment's notice.

PIE FILLINGS

Some flavors naturally work well together, which is why we have so many classic pie recipes. Although you can tweak the combinations and add your own personal touches, there is just no point deviating too far from those classic combinations, as you know when you combine certain ingredients the pie is going to taste great. For example, apple and blackberry, rhubarb and ginger, beef and ale, chicken and mushroom, and turkey and ham are all tried and tested filling combinations that will work every time.

The classic fillings are also some of the easiest to make. What could be simpler than stewing chopped baking apples with sugar and popping in a handful of blackberries at the last minute? Likewise, sautéing chopped chicken and mushrooms and stirring in a little stock and flour is all you need for a tasty chicken pie filling. Obviously, you will want to explore some more unusual combinations, but it's good to have a range of staples that are quick and easy—ideal for everyday meals.

QUANTITIES

When it comes to calculating how much filling you require, it depends on the size of pie pan you are using and how deep it is. With regard to fruits and vegetables, a lot of volume is lost during cooking when the moisture evaporates, so it may seem like you are preparing more than you need, but the amount will shrink down considerably. For a 9-inch pie pan, you will need about 5 cups of prepared fruits or vegetables (pits and cores removed and fruits or vegetables peeled and chopped).

BASIC TECHNIQUES

If you follow the recipes carefully, you should enjoy perfect pies with every attempt. But if pies are going to become a new staple in your culinary repertoire, it makes sense to get to grips with some of the basic techniques used in many of the recipes.

RUBBING IN PASTRY

There are a couple of important points to remember when making pastry—first, you should sift the flour into the bowl to get rid of any lumps; and second, use chilled fat. It also helps if you cut or break the fat into smaller pieces, as this starts the mixing process immediately.

When cutting in the fat with your fingertips, rub the fat into the flour, circulating it around the bowl for air flow. You are aiming for a light, crumbly mixture that doesn't have any large lumps in it, although smaller lumps are fine, as they help to give the pastry a flaky texture. Alternatively, use a pastry blender or pulse in a food processor to incorporate the fat evenly.

ROLLING OUT PASTRY
Always chill pastry in the fridge for about 30 minutes before you are ready to assemble the pie. This helps to dry out the pastry and stop it sticking to work surfaces and rolling pins. Flour the surface lightly and roll the pastry out from the center to the edges, turning it regularly to ensure an even thickness all over. You should aim for a diameter that is larger than the pie pan so there is room to trim and neaten the lid.

PREPARING THE PIE
BLIND BAKING
As previously mentioned, it is important to chill the pastry before baking, and also to let the filling cool completely. If your pie calls for a pastry lining—as well as a lid—this should be blind baked first so the pastry doesn't go soggy as soon as the filling is added. Line the pastry shell with wax paper and half-fill with dry beans, or rice or pie weights, or prick the bottom with a fork so the pastry doesn't blister.

The length of time required to blind bake will depend on the recipe, and also on personal preference. You can either partially bake the shell for a few minutes in a hot oven, or fully bake it for around 15–20 minutes, or until you see the side of the pastry begin to brown around the sides of the pie pan.

ASSEMBLING THE PIE
- Ensure the pie filling is completely cool before filling the pie dish.
- Cut some of the excess pastry into thin strips. Brush the rim of the pie pan with water or egg yolk and use these strips to cover the rim. Now brush the top of this pastry rim with water.
- Carefully roll the pastry pie lid onto the floured rolling pin and position it over the pie, unrolling it so it sits in position over the edges of the pan.
- Trim the extra pastry from around the rim and push down around the edges to keep the pastry firmly in place (see page 10 for crimping tips).
- Brush all over the pie crust with a little beaten egg (or milk), which will help the pastry to turn a rich, golden color.
- Finally, make a small hole in the center of the pie to let the steam escape.

DECORATING

Some pies call for specific decorations, but many people have their own favorite finishing touches. Below are some easy techniques that transform any pie into a centerpiece.

CRIMPING

This is a classic decoration that looks great and has the added practical purpose of keeping the pastry lid firmly secured to the pie bottom. To do this, use the index finger of one hand to make a dent in the crust while pushing back the pastry around it with the index finger and thumb of your other hand.

LATTICE TOP

This is a decorative woven design that works particularly well with fruit pies such as cherry or summer fruits. There are a number of different methods for creating a lattice top—below is one that is easy to follow. If you are short of time, you can simply lay half the strips in one direction and the other half over the top in the other direction. It won't have quite the same impact as a woven lattice but the effect will still be striking.

1. First, roll out the pastry for the pie lid, as you would normally do.

2. Using a knife or pastry wheel, cut the pastry into long strips of even width.

3. Take one strip and place it across the center of the pie, with the ends trailing over the edge of the pie crust.

4. Place another strip over the first to form a cross shape across the pie.

5. Now take the third strip of pastry and begin "weaving." Lay it over the pie, but lift the perpendicular strip of pastry so this now falls over the new strip.

6. Keep working in this way, alternating between the directions of the strips, and lifting those opposite to create the woven effect.

7. When you have covered the pie in the lattice top, trim around the crust and brush the pastry strips with beaten egg.

PASTRY LEAVES

There is always a little pastry left over from the trimmings and this is perfect for pastry leaves or other decorations. Pastry leaves are easy to make and give your pie a finishing flourish.

1. Cut out a selection of leaf shapes.

2. Use a knife or pastry tool to create the markings on the leaf.

3. Brush a little water onto the base of the leaves to help them stick.

4. Position the leaves on the pie crust, then brush the whole crust with beaten egg.

5. Remember to cut a steam hole into the center of the pie.

BAKING TIPS

Transfer your pie pan onto a preheated cookie sheet. This will help to start cooking the pie from underneath as soon as it's in the oven, which should avoid any soggy pastry issues. Transfer the pie into a preheated oven and set a timer so all your hard work isn't wasted by overcooking the pie. It's worth checking on the pie a few minutes before the end of the cooking time, as ovens vary.

Some pies are served warm, others cool, and some completely cold—check the recipe for specific instructions and transfer the pie pan to a wire rack to let cool, if required.

TOP TEN TIPS

1. Use cold ingredients when making the pastry.

2. Chill the dough in the fridge before use.

3. Don't overroll the pastry or it will toughen.

4. Cut the pastry lid bigger than the pie dish.

5. Use a rolling pin to transfer the pastry to the pie dish.

6. Blind bake the pie shell.

7. Cover the edges of the pie crust with foil to prevent burning.

8. Brush the pie lid with beaten egg.

9. Cook in a preheated oven on a preheated cookie sheet.

10. Double check the oven temperature and cooking times.

MAKING PASTRY

BASICS

SHORT-CRUST PASTRY

The classic choice for savory and sweet pies, short-crust pastry is easy to handle and holds its shape well for pie shells.

MAKES ABOUT 10½ OZ
- 1½ cups plus 2 tablespoons all-purpose flour, plus extra for dusting
- Pinch of salt
- 7 tablespoons (½ stick plus 3 tablespoons) fat, such as equal quantities of butter and vegetable shortening, chilled
- 2–3 tablespoons ice water

1. Sift the flour and salt into a bowl or food processor. Cut the fat into small pieces and add it to the flour.

2. Cut the fat into the flour with a pastry blender or the fingertips or pulse with the food processor until the mixture resembles fine bread crumbs.

3. Sprinkle the ice water over the surface and stir with a palette knife until the mixture begins to clump together or pulse briefly in the food processor.

4. Turn out the pastry onto a lightly floured work surface and press it together lightly with the fingers. Chill for about 30 minutes before use.

RICH SHORT-CRUST PASTRY

The inclusion of an egg yolk gives a fine, crisp pastry ideal for sweet pies, but it can also be used for savory pies if you need a standing crust.

MAKES ABOUT 10½ OZ
- 1½ cups plus 2 tablespoons all-purpose flour, plus extra for dusting
- Pinch of salt
- 7 tablespoons (½ stick plus 3 tablespoons) fat, such as equal quantities of butter and vegetable shortening, chilled
- 1 large egg yolk
- 2–3 tablespoons ice water if needed

1. Sift the flour and salt into a bowl. Cut the fat into small pieces and add it to the flour.

2. Cut the fat into the flour with a pastry blender or the fingertips or pulse with the food processor until the mixture resembles fine bread crumbs.

3. Add the egg yolk and stir with a palette knife until the mixture begins to clump together or pulse briefly in the food processor, then mix in just enough ice water if necessary to make a firm dough.

4. Turn out the pastry onto a lightly floured work surface and press it together lightly with the fingers. Chill for about 30 minutes before use.

PÂTE
SUCRÉE

A sweet, enriched short pastry, this has a cookie-like texture suitable for sweet pies. This makes enough dough to line an 8-inch tart pan.

MAKES ABOUT 10½ OZ

- 1⅓ cups plus 1 tablespoon all-purpose flour
- Pinch of salt
- ⅓ cup (½ stick plus 1⅓ tablespoons) unsalted butter, slightly softened
- 2 large egg yolks
- 1 tablespoon ice water
- 3 tablespoons superfine sugar

1. Sift the flour and salt into a pile on a cold work surface and make a well in the center.

2. Add the butter, egg yolks, ice water, and sugar to the well and use the fingertips of one hand to work them together into a rough paste. The mixture should resemble scrambled egg.

3. Gradually work in the flour with your fingertips to bind the mixture into a smooth dough. Press together lightly and form into a ball. Wrap in foil and chill for about 30 minutes before use.

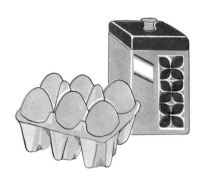

PUFF PASTRY

Well-made puff pastry will rise to about six times its height when it is cooked. Although it has a reputation for being difficult to make, the most important guideline is to keep all the ingredients cool.

MAKES ABOUT 1½ LB
- 2 cups all-purpose flour, plus extra for dusting
- Pinch of salt
- 1 cup plus 2 tablespoons butter in one piece, chilled
- 1 teaspoon lemon juice
- ⅔ cup ice water

1. Sift the flour and salt into a bowl. Cut a quarter of the butter into the flour with a pastry blender or the fingertips until the mixture resembles bread crumbs. Add the lemon juice and most of the ice water. Mix to a dough and gradually add the rest of the water to form a dry dough.

2. Knead the dough into a ball on a floured work surface, then flatten. Wrap in foil and chill for about 30 minutes.

3. Put the rest of the butter between two sheets of plastic wrap and roll out to a square about ½ inch thick. Unwrap the chilled pastry and roll it out to form a square large enough to wrap around the butter. Put the butter in the center of the pastry square and fold over the edges to encase the butter completely.

4. Dust the work surface and rolling pin and roll out the pastry to a long rectangle about ½ inch thick. Fold the bottom third onto the middle third, then fold the top third over the top. Rewrap and chill for 15 minutes.

5. Return the pastry to the work surface with a short edge facing toward you. Press down on the edges slightly, then roll it out into a rectangle and fold as before. Repeat this six times, then chill the pastry. Roll it out to its final shape, then chill again for 30 minutes. "Scallop" the pastry edges by holding the back of a knife blade horizontally to the pastry edge and tapping it, so the layers rise properly.

ROUGH PUFF PASTRY

This deliciously rich and crisp, slightly flaky pastry is ideal for single-crust pies, turnovers, or sweet pastries. It does not rise as much as puff pastry, but it's far simpler to make.

MAKES ABOUT 1¼ LB
- 2 cups all-purpose flour, plus extra for dusting
- Pinch of salt
- ¾ cup (1½ sticks) butter, chilled until almost frozen
- About ⅔ cup ice water mixed with 2 teaspoons lemon juice

1. Sift the flour and salt into a bowl. Holding the butter with cool fingertips or by its folded-back wrapper, shred it directly over the flour. Work quickly before the butter softens from the heat of your hand.

2. Stir the butter into the flour with a palette knife, then sprinkle with just enough ice water to start binding the ingredients into a dough. Press the dough lightly together with your fingertips.

3. Turn out the dough onto a lightly floured work surface and roll it out into a rectangle about three times longer than it is wide.

4. Fold the bottom third of the pastry up and the top third down, then press around the sides with a rolling pin to seal the layers together lightly. Chill for about 30 minutes before use.

POTATO PASTRY

A rougher pastry that doesn't need much rolling out, this is great when used to line pie dishes for rustic pies.

MAKES ABOUT 26 OZ
- 10 oz mealy potatoes, peeled and diced
- 2 cups all-purpose flour, plus extra for dusting
- ½ cup plus 1 tablespoon (1 stick plus 1 tablespoon) slightly salted butter, cut into small pieces
- ⅓ cup (½ stick plus 1⅓ tablespoons) shortening, cut into small pieces
- 1–2 tablespoons ice water
- Salt

1. In a saucepan, cook the diced potato in salted boiling water until tender, 8–10 minutes. Drain well and return to the pan. Mash until smooth and let cool.

2. Sift the flour into a bowl or food processor. Add the butter and shortening and cut in with a pastry blender or the fingertips or pulse with the food processor until the mixture resembles bread crumbs.

3. Add the potato, cutting it into the flour with a knife. Add 1 tablespoon ice water and mix to a smooth dough or pulse briefly in the food processor, mixing in a dash more water if the dough feels dry.

4. Turn out onto a lightly floured work surface and bring the mixture together to form a smooth ball of dough. Wrap in foil and chill for at least 1 hour before use.

HOT WATER CRUST PASTRY

This traditional pastry is made in a completely different way from other pie dough, by warming shortening in milk, then mixing it into flour.

MAKES ABOUT 1½ LB
- ¾ cup (1½ sticks) shortening
- ¾ cup milk or half milk and half water
- 3 cups all-purpose flour, plus extra for dusting
- ¼ teaspoon salt

1. In a saucepan, gently heat the shortening and milk or milk and water mix until the shortening has just melted. Bring just to a boil, then tip into a bowl containing the flour and salt and mix with a wooden spoon until it forms a smooth soft ball.

2. Cover the top of the bowl with a clean dish towel and let stand until cool enough to handle, 10–20 minutes.

3. Knead the dough briefly on a lightly floured work surface, then shape and bake according to the chosen recipe.

CHOUX PASTRY

This breaks all the rules for pastry making—it needs lots of heat and firm handling for good results. Use it to make a bun topping or ring for a sweet pie, or for cream-filled buns (see page 150).

MAKES ABOUT 10½ OZ
- ½ cup plus 2 tablespoons all-purpose flour
- Pinch of salt
- 4 tablespoons (½ stick) unsalted butter
- ⅔ cup water or half milk and half water
- 2 extra-large eggs, lightly beaten

1. Sift the flour and salt onto a sheet of wax paper.

2. In a saucepan, gently heat the butter and water or milk and water mix until the butter has just melted, then bring to a boil. Don't bring to a boil before the butter has melted.

3. Remove the pan from the heat and immediately add the flour, all at once. Beat with a wooden spoon or electric hand mixer just until the mixture forms a smooth ball that leaves the sides of the pan clean. Don't overbeat at this stage or the paste will become oily.

4. Let the mixture cool for 2 minutes. Gradually add the eggs, beating hard after each addition, and continue to beat until the mixture is smooth and glossy. The paste should be just soft enough to fall gently from the spoon. Use the pastry right away or cover closely and chill until needed.

CRÈME PATISSIÈRE

Use this thick, creamy custard as a filling for a pie shell, piling it with soft fruits to make a fabulous summer pie. Alternatively, pack it into choux buns instead of whipped cream (see page 150). The quantities can easily be doubled.

SERVES 4-6
- ⅔ cup milk
- ⅔ cup heavy cream
- 1 vanilla bean
- 4 large egg yolks
- 3 tablespoons superfine sugar
- 2 tablespoons all-purpose flour

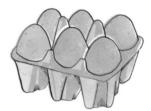

1. In a heavy-bottom pan, combine the milk and cream. Use the tip of a small, sharp knife to score the vanilla bean lengthwise through to the center. Add it to the pan and bring the mixture to a boil. Remove the pan from the heat and let infuse for 20 minutes.

2. In a large bowl, beat the egg yolks, sugar, and flour together until smooth. Remove the vanilla bean from the milk, scrape out the seeds with the tip of a knife, and return them to the milk. Pour the milk over the egg mixture, beating well.

3. Return the custard to the pan and cook over gentle heat, stirring continuously with a wooden spoon, until it is thick and smooth, 4-5 minutes. Turn the custard into a small bowl and cover with wax paper to prevent a skin from forming. Let cool before use.

CRÈME ANGLAISE

- -

The perfect sauce for pouring over a wedge of fruit pie. Don't be tempted to cook the custard over high heat or it might curdle. The bay leaves or rosemary sprigs are not essential, but they do provide a delicious flavor that complements the vanilla.

SERVES 6

- 1 vanilla bean
- 3 bay leaves or 3 rosemary sprigs
- 1⅓ cups milk
- 1⅓ cups light cream
- 6 large egg yolks
- 2 tablespoons superfine sugar

1. Use the tip of a small, sharp knife to score the vanilla bean lengthwise through to the center. In a heavy-bottom pan, combine the vanilla bean with the bay leaves or rosemary, milk, and cream and bring the mixture slowly to a boil. Remove the pan from the heat and let infuse for 20 minutes.

2. In a large bowl, beat the egg yolks and sugar together. Remove the herb and vanilla bean from the milk, scrape out the seeds of the vanilla bean with the tip of a knife, and return them to the milk.

3. Pour the milk over the eggs and sugar, beating well. Return the mixture to the cleaned pan and cook over very gentle heat, stirring continuously with a wooden spoon, until the sauce is thick enough to coat the back of the spoon, up to 10 minutes. Pour the sauce into a pitcher and serve warm.

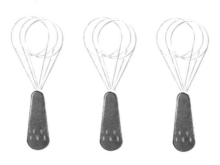

VANILLA SABAYON

Served warm or cold, sabayon sauce makes a lovely summer dessert when it is spooned over a freshly baked fruit pie.

SERVES 3-4

- 4 large egg yolks
- 2 tablespoons Vanilla Sugar (see Tip)
- I teaspoon vanilla extract
- 2 tablespoons Marsala

1. In a large heatproof bowl, combine the egg yolks, vanilla sugar, vanilla extract, and Marsala. Set the bowl over a saucepan of gently simmering water, making sure the bottom of the bowl doesn't come into contact with the water.

2. Whip with an electric hand mixer or wire whip until pale, creamy, and thick enough for the beaters to leave a trail when lifted from the bowl.

3. If you are serving the sauce hot, use it right away. If it is to be served cold, remove the bowl from the heat and beat until it is cool, an additional 2-3 minutes. Let the sauce stand for up to 10 minutes before serving.

TIP

- To make vanilla sugar, rinse a vanilla bean and pat dry thoroughly with paper towels, then insert into a jar or other airtight container of superfine sugar. Store for about 2 weeks before using, shaking the container from time to time.

SOUR CREAM & CHIVE ROASTED VEGETABLES

Serve this vegetable medley and dipping sauce to accompany a freshly baked savory pie of your choice for a welcoming winter feast.

SERVES 4

- 2 lb mixed winter vegetables, such as carrots, parsnips, rutabaga, and turnips
- 12 new potatoes, scrubbed and halved if large
- 2 small onions, cut into wedges
- 12 garlic cloves, unpeeled
- Handful of thyme and rosemary sprigs
- 3 bay leaves
- Extra virgin olive oil, for drizzling
- Salt and black pepper

Sauce
- 1¼ cups sour cream
- 1 bunch of chives, snipped

1. Preheat the oven to 450°F. Peel and trim the vegetables, then cut them into pieces, keeping them about the same size as the potatoes so they cook evenly.

2. In a large roasting pan, combine the vegetables, potatoes, onions, garlic cloves, and herbs, and season with salt and pepper. Drizzle generously with olive oil and toss until well coated with the oil. Roast in the oven for 50-60 minutes, stirring from time to time, until the vegetables are tender.

3. Meanwhile, make the sauce. In a bowl, mix the sour cream and chives together, and season with salt and pepper. Cover and chill until needed.

4. Serve the roasted vegetables with the sauce for dipping.

BRAISED FENNEL WITH PECORINO

Serve the fennel and pan juices along with some boiled new potatoes as the ideal complement to a seafood or vegetable pie.

SERVES 4
- 4 tablespoons (½ stick) butter
- 12 baby fennel bulbs, trimmed and halved lengthwise
- ⅔ cup water
- Squeeze of lemon juice
- 1 teaspoon balsamic vinegar
- 3–4 tablespoons freshly grated pecorino cheese
- Salt and black pepper

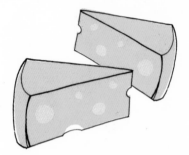

1. In a large flameproof casserole dish, melt the butter and when it stops foaming add the fennel halves and cook gently until lightly golden, 2 minutes each side.

2. Add the water and lemon juice, season with salt and pepper, and bring to a boil. Cover and simmer gently until the fennel is tender, 20 minutes.

3. Remove the lid, add the vinegar, and increase the heat to reduce the liquid by half. Remove from the heat, add the cheese, then re-cover to let the cheese melt.

CHEESY MUSTARD MASH & ROASTED TOMATOES

SERVES 4-6

- 1½ lb mealy potatoes, peeled and cut into small chunks
- Large pat of butter
- 4 tablespoons milk
- 1 small garlic clove, crushed
- 2¼ cups shredded cheddar cheese
- 1 tablespoon whole grain mustard
- Salt and black pepper

Roasted tomatoes
- 1 lb small tomatoes on the vine
- 1 tablespoon chopped rosemary
- 1 teaspoon sugar
- Olive oil, for drizzling

1. Preheat the oven to 400°F. Place the tomatoes still on the vine in a shallow ovenproof dish and sprinkle with the rosemary and sugar. Drizzle with olive oil and season generously with salt and pepper. Roast in the oven for 15-20 minutes, until lightly charred.

2. Meanwhile, in a saucepan, cook the potatoes in lightly salted boiling water until tender, about 10 minutes. Drain well and return to the pan. Mash with the butter until smooth.

3. Return the pan to the heat and stir in the milk and garlic. Season with salt and pepper and beat gently with a wooden spoon. Gradually beat in the cheese and mustard and continue to beat over low heat until the mixture lightens, becomes glossy, and starts to pull away from the sides of the pan. Serve the mash with the roasted tomatoes to accompany the freshly baked pie of your choice.

GRAVY

Roasted meat or poultry provide delicious fats and meat juices for a
well-flavored gravy to serve with your favorite pie. Simply pour from the
roasting pan into a bowl and let cool, then cover and chill. Discard most
or all of the solidified fat before using.

SERVES 4-6
- Drippings reserved from roasted meat
- 1 tablespoon all-purpose flour
  (less for a thin gravy)
- 1¼–1⅔ cups liquid (this could be vegetable
  cooking water, stock, half stock and half water,
  or half wine and half water)
- Salt and black pepper

1. In a pan, warm the drippings, sprinkle in the flour, and cook
over medium heat, stirring with a wooden spoon, for 1 minute.

2. Gradually blend the liquid into
the mixture and bring to a boil,
stirring well. Reduce the heat and
cook gently until the gravy is thick
and glossy. Check the seasoning,
adding salt and pepper as
necessary. Strain into a pitcher.

TIP

- For lamb or game gravy, a
spoonful of red currant jelly adds
a subtle sweetness. For pork, try
apple jelly and hard cider instead
of stock. To sharpen up a rich, fatty
gravy, add a squeeze of lemon juice.
A teaspoon of mustard makes a
good addition to beef gravy.

RED WINE GRAVY

Some sliced onion, garlic, and herb sprigs placed under meat or poultry for roasting will enhance the flavor of the reserved meat drippings to use for gravy.

SERVES 6

- Drippings reserved from roasted meat
- 2 teaspoons all-purpose flour
- 1¼ cups beef or lamb stock
- ⅔ cup full-bodied red wine
- Salt and black pepper

1. In a pan, warm the drippings, sprinkle in the flour, and cook over medium heat, stirring with a wooden spoon, for 1 minute.

2. Gradually blend the stock and wine into the mixture and bring to a boil, stirring well. Reduce the heat and cook gently until the gravy is slightly thickened and glossy. Check the seasoning, add salt and pepper if needed. Strain into a pitcher.

TIP

- To make a chicken gravy, use chicken stock and white wine instead of the red. Other flavorings such as ground cumin and coriander and red currant jelly can be added to lamb gravy. Mustard or horseradish sauce are good with beef.

FESTIVE GAME PIE P48

SAVORY PIES

SAUSAGE PIE WITH CELERY ROOT MASH

- - - - - - - - - - - - - - - - -

SERVES 4

- 8 pork link sausages
- 4 tablespoons (½ stick) butter
- 1 tablespoon vegetable oil
- 2 onions, sliced
- 1 large fennel bulb, trimmed and chopped
- 2 tablespoons all-purpose flour
- 1⅔ cups pork or chicken stock
- 1 teaspoon fennel seed, lightly crushed
- Several sage leaves, chopped
- 1½ lb celery root, peeled and cut into chunks
- 1¼ lb mealy potatoes, peeled and cut into chunks
- 2–3 tablespoons milk
- ½ cup shredded Gruyère cheese
- Salt and black pepper

1. Preheat the oven to 350°F. Cut each sausage into four or five pieces. In a skillet, melt half the butter with the oil and gently brown the sausage on all sides. Drain to a pie dish.

2. Add the onions and fennel and cook gently until softened and pale golden, about 10 minutes. Sprinkle in the flour and cook, stirring, for 1 minute. Gradually blend in the stock and bring to a boil. Cook, stirring, for 2 minutes. Remove from the heat and add the fennel seed and sage. Season to taste and spoon over the sausage.

3. In saucepan, cook the celery root and potatoes in boiling water until tender, 10–15 minutes. Drain well and return to the pan. Mash with the remaining butter, salt and pepper, and enough milk to give a light and fluffy mash. Spoon over the filling and fluff up the surface with a fork. Sprinkle with the cheese. Bake in the oven for about 45 minutes, until the surface is crusty and golden.

MEDIEVAL SPICED STEAK PIES

These are delicious served as an appetizer before the Thanksgiving or Christmas roast turkey, or a special roast dinner.

MAKES 24

- Single quantity Short-Crust Pastry (see page 14), chilled
- Butter, for greasing
- All-purpose flour, for dusting
- Beaten egg, to glaze
- Sifted confectioners' sugar, for dusting

Filling
- ⅓ cup brandy
- ⅔ cup currants
- ⅔ cup raisins
- 1½ oz candied or preserved ginger, chopped
- Grated zest of ½ orange
- Grated zest of ½ lemon
- ½ teaspoon apple pie spice
- ¼ teaspoon grated nutmeg
- ⅔ cup chopped blanched almonds
- 7 oz extra-lean ground beef
- ¾ cup shredded suet or shortening
- 1 tart apple, cored and grated

1. Make the filling. In a saucepan, bring the brandy just to a boil and add the dried fruits, ginger, citrus zest, and spices, then let cool. Mix in the almonds, beef, shredded suet or shortening, and apple, then cover and refrigerate overnight so the flavors can develop.

2. Next day, preheat the oven to 375°F. Grease a standard-size 12-cup muffin/cupcake pan. Roll out two-thirds of the pastry on a lightly floured work surface and use a 3-inch plain cookie cutter to cut 12 circles, rerolling the trimmings. Press into the cups of the pan, then spoon in the filling.

3. Roll out the reserved pastry with any trimmings and use a 2½-inch plain cookie cutter to cut out 24 circles for the pie tops, rerolling the trimmings as needed. Brush the top edges of the pie shells with beaten egg, add the lids, and press the edges together firmly to seal. Brush the tops with beaten egg, then make 4 small steam vents in each pie. Bake in the oven for 15 minutes, until the pie crust is golden. Let stand for 10 minutes, then loosen the edges of the pastry and transfer to a wire rack to cool. Just before serving, dust the tops lightly with sifted confectioners' sugar.

STEAK & MUSHROOM PIE

- - - - - - - - - - - - - - - - - - -

The filling is cooked a day in advance, as you need to let it cool completely before adding the pastry lid, but it also helps to enhance the flavor.

SERVES 4

- 3 tablespoons all-purpose flour, plus extra for dusting
- 4 tablespoons (½ stick) butter
- 1½ lb beef stew meat, diced
- 1 large onion, chopped
- 2 garlic cloves, crushed
- 1¾ cups stout
- ⅔ cup beef stock
- 2 bay leaves
- 1 tablespoon hot horseradish sauce
- ½ lb button mushrooms
- Single quantity Short-Crust Pastry (see page 14), chilled
- Milk, to glaze
- Salt and black pepper

1. Preheat the oven to 300°F. Season the flour with salt and pepper and use it to coat the steak. In a large, heavy-bottom skillet, melt a pat of the butter and brown the beef on all sides in batches, lifting the batches out with a slotted spoon into a casserole dish. Add a little more butter to the skillet and sauté the onion and garlic until softened.

2. Add the stout, stock, bay leaves, horseradish sauce, and salt and pepper to the skillet. Bring to a boil, then pour over the beef. Cover and cook in the oven for 1½ hours, until the beef is tender.

3. Meanwhile, add the remaining butter to the skillet and sauté the mushrooms for 5 minutes, then add them to the beef mix for the last 30 minutes of the cooking time. Let cool, then turn the beef mix into a 7-cup pie dish, cover, and chill.

4. Preheat the oven to 375°F. Roll out the pastry on a lightly floured work surface until it is slightly larger than the dish and use to cover the pie (see page 9). Brush the pastry with milk, make a hole in the center of the pie, and bake in the oven for 45 minutes, until the pie crust is deep golden.

STEAK & KIDNEY PIE

Again, as the meat filling needs to be cooled before being topped with pastry, it may be easier to cook it the day before, let cool, and chill overnight, ready to fill the pie.

SERVES 6

- 1½ lb chuck steak, cubed
- ½ lb beef kidney, cores removed and trimmed
- 1 large onion, chopped
- 1 celery stalk, chopped
- 2 carrots, chopped
- 1¼ cups water
- ½ teaspoon dried thyme
- 1 tablespoon soy sauce
- 1 tablespoon cornstarch
- 2 tablespoons chopped fresh parsley
- ¾ lb puff pastry (see page 17 for homemade), thawed if frozen but chilled
- All-purpose flour, for dusting
- Salt and black pepper
- Beaten egg, to glaze

1. In a large saucepan, combine the steak, kidney, onion, celery, and carrots. Add the water, thyme, soy sauce, and salt and pepper. Bring to a boil, then cover and simmer until the meat is tender, about 1½ hours.

2. Taste and add more seasoning if necessary. In a cup, blend the cornstarch to a paste with some water. Stir into the pan and cook, stirring, until the meat sauce is thickened and smooth. Stir in the parsley and cool.

3. Preheat the oven to 425°F. Roll out half the pastry on a lightly floured work surface and use to line a 5-cup ovenproof dish or a 9-inch pie plate, letting it extend slightly over the top edges. Spoon the cooled meat mixture into the pie shell. Brush the top edges of the pastry with beaten egg. Roll out the remaining pastry and trimmings to 2 inches larger than the dish and position on top (see page 9). Press the pastry edges together firmly to seal, trim off the excess, then crimp the edges (see page 10) or press with a fork. Make pastry leaves with the trimmings (see page 11).

4. Brush the pastry with beaten egg, make a hole in the center of the pie, and bake in the oven for 35–40 minutes, until the pie crust is crisp and golden brown. Serve hot with mashed potatoes and green vegetables such as cabbage or Brussels sprouts.

BEEF GUINNESS PIE

SERVES 6

- 2 tablespoons vegetable oil
- 2 lb chuck steak, cubed
- 2 onions, thinly sliced
- 2 celery stalks, chopped
- 3 tablespoons all-purpose flour
- 1¾ cups Guinness
- ⅔ cup beef stock
- 2 teaspoons light brown sugar
- 2 bay leaves
- 2 teaspoons Worcestershire sauce
- 1 tablespoon tomato paste
- ⅔ cup pitted prunes
- Salt and black pepper

Pastry
- 1⅓ cups plus 1 tablespoon all-purpose flour, plus extra for dusting
- ¼ cup finely chopped walnuts
- 1 teaspoon mustard seed
- ½ cup plus 1 tablespoon (1 stick plus 1 tablespoon) butter, chilled and diced
- 2–3 tablespoons ice water
- Beaten egg, to glaze

1. In a large saucepan, heat the oil and brown the steak on all sides. Add the onions and celery and sauté until browned, about 5 minutes. Stir in the flour and cook, stirring, for 1 minute.

2. Gradually blend in the Guinness and stock and cook, stirring, until thickened and smooth. Stir in the remaining ingredients with salt and pepper to taste. Cover the pan and simmer until the meat is tender, about 1½ hours. Pour into a 1½-quart pie dish and let cool slightly.

3. Preheat the oven to 375°F. Make the pastry. Sift the flour and a bit of salt into a bowl or food processor and mix in the walnuts and mustard seed. Add the butter and cut in with a pastry blender or the fingertips or pulse with the food processor until the mixture resembles fine bread crumbs. Add enough ice water to mix or pulse to a firm dough.

4. Knead the dough briefly on a lightly floured work surface. Roll out until it is slightly larger than the dish and use to cover the pie (see page 9), then crimp the edges (see page 10). Brush the pastry with beaten egg, make a hole in the center of the pie, and bake in the oven for 35–40 minutes, until the pie crust is crisp and golden brown. Serve hot with a green vegetable.

CRUSTY SHEPHERD'S PIE

SERVES 4-6

- 1 tablespoon olive oil
- 4 smoked bacon slices, chopped
- 1 onion, chopped
- 1 lb ground lamb
- 1 teaspoon dried oregano
- 2 tablespoons chopped parsley
- ⅔ cup red wine
- 1⅔ cup strained tomatoes
- Salt and black pepper

Scone topping
- 2 cups self-rising flour, plus extra for dusting
- 4 tablespoons (½ stick) butter, chilled and diced, plus extra for greasing
- 2 teaspoons whole grain mustard
- ⅔ cup shredded sharp cheddar cheese
- ½ cup milk

1. In a skillet, heat the oil and gently cook the bacon and onion until softened, about 5 minutes. Add the lamb and cook, stirring, until evenly browned.

2. Stir in the herbs, wine, and strained tomatoes with salt and pepper to taste. Bring to a boil, then simmer, uncovered, until the lamb is tender and the sauce thickened, about 25 minutes.

3. Preheat the oven to 400°F. Grease a 5-cup pie dish. Make the scone topping. Sift the flour into a bowl or food processor and season with salt and pepper. Add the butter and cut in with a pastry blender or the fingertips or pulse with the food processor until the mixture resembles fine bread crumbs. Mix in the mustard and a scant ½ cup of the cheese, then add enough of the milk to mix or pulse to a soft dough.

4. Knead the dough briefly on a lightly floured surface, then roll out to a thickness of ½ inch. Use a 2-inch cookie cutter to cut into circles. Reroll the trimmings and cut out more circles.

5. Transfer the meat mixture to the pie dish. Arrange the scones over the top, brush with milk, and sprinkle with the remaining cheese. Bake in the oven for 25 minutes, until the topping is golden brown. Serve hot.

MOROCCAN-STYLE
LAMB PIE

SERVES 5-6

- 4 garlic cloves, coarsely chopped
- 2 oz fresh ginger, peeled and coarsely chopped
- ½ teaspoon crushed red pepper
- ⅓ cup coarsely chopped cilantro
- Several mint sprigs, coarsely chopped
- 1 tablespoon ras-el-hanout spice mix
- 2½ lb boneless lean lamb shoulder or loin, diced
- 5 tablespoons olive oil
- 2 onions, chopped
- 3 carrots, sliced
- 2 tablespoons all-purpose flour
- 1½ cups lamb or chicken stock
- 1 tablespoon clear honey
- 1 cup coarsely chopped pitted dried dates
- 1 teaspoon orange blossom water
- 5 sheets of phyllo dough, thawed if frozen but chilled
- Sea salt

1. Preheat the oven to 350°F. In a food processor, blend the garlic, ginger, red pepper, cilantro, mint, and spice mix to a paste. (Alternatively, crush the garlic and finely chop the ginger and herbs.) In a bowl, mix the paste with the lamb, cover, and chill for several hours or overnight.

2. In a flameproof casserole dish, heat 2 tablespoons of the oil and brown the lamb on all sides in batches, lifting the batches out with a slotted spoon onto a plate. Add the onions and carrots to the casserole and sauté gently for 5 minutes. Return the meat to the casserole, sprinkle in the flour, and cook, stirring, for 1 minute. Blend in the stock and bring to a boil. Cover and bake in the oven for 1¼ hours, or until the meat is tender.

3. Remove the casserole from the oven and stir in the honey, dates, orange blossom water, and salt if needed. Transfer to a pie dish and cool.

4. Preheat the oven to 375°F. Lay one sheet of phyllo over the pie, crumpling the pastry so it's not completely flat. Brush with a bit more of the oil and trim off the excess around the edges. Scatter the trimmings over the top. Repeat with the remaining pastry, brushing each layer with oil. Sprinkle with sea salt and bake in the oven for 40 minutes, until the phyllo is golden and the pie is very hot, covering with foil if the pastry begins to overbrown.

LAMB, TOMATO & BASIL PIE

SERVES 4-5

- 1¾ lb boneless leg of lamb, cut into small chunks
- 2 medium eggplants (about 1¼ lb)
- 6 tablespoons olive oil
- 2 onions, thinly sliced
- 3 garlic cloves, crushed
- 28-oz can plum tomatoes
- 2 teaspoons sugar
- ⅔ cup lamb or chicken stock
- 3 tablespoons sun-dried tomato paste
- 2 tablespoons capers
- ⅓ cup packed basil leaves, torn into small pieces
- Double quantity Short-Crust Pastry (see page 14), chilled
- All-purpose flour, for dusting
- Beaten egg, to glaze
- 3 tablespoons freshly grated Parmesan cheese
- Salt and black pepper

1. Season the lamb with salt and pepper. Cut the eggplants into ¾-inch pieces. In a large saucepan, heat 2 tablespoons of the oil and brown the lamb in batches, lifting the batches out with a slotted spoon onto a plate. Heat another 3 tablespoons of the oil and sauté the eggplant, turning frequently, until turning golden, about 10 minutes.

2. Add the onions and garlic to the pan with the remaining oil and sauté for 2–3 minutes. Return the lamb to the pan with the tomatoes, sugar, stock, and tomato paste. Bring to a gentle simmer, cover, and cook very gently until the lamb is tender, 1¼ hours. Season to taste with salt and pepper and stir in the capers and basil. Turn into a pie dish and let cool.

3. Preheat the oven to 375°F. Roll out the pastry on a lightly floured work surface until it is slightly larger than the dish and use to cover the pie (see page 9), then scallop the edges with the back of a knife (see page 17). Brush the pastry with beaten egg, make a hole in the center of the pie, and bake in the oven for 20 minutes. Sprinkle with the Parmesan and bake for another 20 minutes, or until the pie crust is deep golden.

CHORIZO, EGGPLANT & TOMATO PIE

SERVES 4-6

- 1 lb eggplant, cubed
- 2 tablespoons olive oil
- 1 large onion, thinly sliced
- 6 oz chorizo, sliced
- 2 garlic cloves, chopped
- 2 red bell peppers, seeded and chopped
- 14½-oz can diced tomatoes
- 1 tablespoon tomato paste
- Salt and black pepper

Pastry
- 1⅓ cups whole-wheat self-rising flour, plus extra for dusting
- ⅓ cup (½ stick plus 1⅓ tablespoons) butter, chilled and diced
- ¼ cup grated Parmesan cheese
- 2 teaspoons dried oregano
- 1 large egg yolk
- 1–2 tablespoons ice water
- Beaten egg or milk, to glaze

1. Place the eggplant in a colander, sprinkle with salt, and let stand for 30 minutes. Rinse under cold running water, drain, and dry well on paper towels.

2. In a large saucepan, heat the oil and sauté the onion until softened and lightly browned, about 10 minutes. Stir in the chorizo, garlic, and bell peppers and sauté for 5 minutes. Stir in the eggplant, tomatoes, and tomato paste with salt and pepper to taste. Bring to a boil, cover, and simmer for 20 minutes. Let cool, then turn into a 5-cup pie dish.

3. Preheat the oven to 400°F. Make the pastry. Sift the flour into a bowl or food processor. Add the butter and cut in with a pastry blender or the fingertips or pulse with the food processor until the mixture resembles fine bread crumbs. Mix in the Parmesan and oregano, then add the egg yolk and enough ice water to mix or pulse to a firm dough.

4. Knead the dough briefly on a lightly floured work surface, then roll out thinly, cut into strips, and use to create a lattice top for the pie (see page 10). Brush the pastry with beaten egg or milk and bake in the oven for 35–40 minutes, until the pastry is crisp and golden brown. Serve hot.

VEAL, LEMON & TARRAGON PIE

SERVES 5-6

- 3 tablespoons all-purpose flour, plus extra for dusting
- 2 lb veal stew meat, diced
- 4 tablespoons (½ stick) butter
- 2 tablespoons vegetable oil
- 1 onion, chopped
- 1 fennel bulb, trimmed and chopped
- 3 garlic cloves, crushed
- 1⅔ cups chicken stock
- Finely grated zest of 1 lemon
- Leaves from several large tarragon sprigs
- 2 bay leaves
- 1 lb puff pastry (see page 17 for homemade), thawed if frozen but chilled
- Beaten egg, to glaze
- Salt and black pepper

1. Season the flour with salt and pepper and use to coat the veal. In a large saucepan or flameproof casserole dish, melt the butter with the oil and brown the veal on all sides in batches, lifting the batches out with a slotted spoon onto a plate. Add the onion and fennel to the pan and sauté gently for 5 minutes. Stir in the garlic and sauté, stirring, for 1 minute.

2. Tip in any flour left on the plate and blend in the stock. Bring to a boil, then reduce the heat. Return the meat to the pan with the lemon zest, tarragon, and bay leaves, cover, and simmer very gently until the meat is tender, about 1 hour. Let cool, then turn into a pie dish.

3. Preheat the oven to 400°F. Roll out the pastry on a lightly floured work surface until it is slightly larger than the dish and use to cover the pie (see page 9), then scallop the edges with the back of a knife (see page 17). Brush the pastry with beaten egg and sprinkle with plenty of pepper, make a hole in the center of the pie, and bake in the oven for 30–40 minutes, until the pie crust is deep golden.

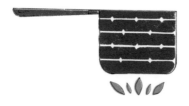

RABBIT PIE

SERVES 5-6

- 3 tablespoons all-purpose flour, plus extra for dusting
- 1¾ lb boneless lean rabbit, diced
- 4 tablespoons (½ stick) butter
- 2 tablespoons vegetable oil
- 2 onions, chopped
- 2 carrots, diced
- 3 garlic cloves, crushed
- 1 tablespoon chopped rosemary
- 8 juniper berries, lightly crushed
- 1 ⅔ cups game or chicken stock
- Double quantity Short-Crust Pastry (see page 14), chilled
- Beaten egg, to glaze
- Salt and black pepper

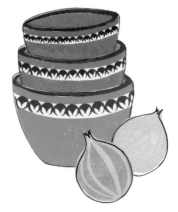

1. Preheat the oven to 325°F. Season the flour with salt and pepper and use to coat the rabbit. In a skillet, melt the butter with the oil and brown the rabbit on all sides in batches, lifting the batches out with a slotted spoon into a casserole dish. Add the onions and carrots to the pan and sauté until softened, about 5 minutes, adding the garlic for the last couple of minutes.

2. Tip in any flour left on the plate and add the rosemary and juniper berries. Blend in the stock and bring to a boil. Pour over the rabbit in the casserole, cover, and cook in the oven for 1 hour. Check the seasoning and let cool, then turn into a pie dish.

3. Preheat the oven to 400°F. Roll out the pastry on a lightly floured work surface until it is slightly larger than the dish and use to cover the pie (see page 9), then scallop the edges with the back of a knife (see page 17). Brush the pastry with beaten egg, make a hole in the center of the pie, and bake in the oven for 30–40 minutes, until the pie crust is deep golden.

FESTIVE GAME PIE

Perfect for making ahead, this pie will sit well in the fridge overnight, ready to pop in the oven. Reheat any remaining stock and serve in a pitcher.

SERVES 6

- 14 oz sausage meat
- 2 onions, finely chopped
- 2 teaspoons chopped thyme
- ⅓ cup (½ stick plus 1⅓ tablespoons) butter
- 14 oz lean turkey, diced
- 4 pigeon breasts, sliced
- 1 lb pheasant meat, diced
- 2 celery stalks, thinly sliced
- 3 garlic cloves, crushed
- 3 tablespoons all-purpose flour, plus extra for dusting
- 3¾ cups game or chicken stock
- 1⅓ cups cooked peeled chestnuts
- Double quantity Short-Crust Pastry (see page 14)
- Beaten egg, to glaze
- Salt and black pepper

1. Mix the sausage meat with 1 onion and a little thyme. (This is best done with your hands.) Shape into 18 small balls. In a skillet, melt 2 tablespoons of the butter and cook the meatballs on all sides until golden. Lift out with a slotted spoon onto a plate. Cook the meats in batches until golden, and add more butter to the pan if needed. Lift the batches out onto the plate.

2. Add the remaining butter to the pan and sauté the remaining onion and the celery until softened, about 5 minutes. Add the garlic and cook, stirring, for 1 minute. Stir in the flour, then gradually blend in the stock and bring to a boil, stirring. Cook for 4–5 minutes. Mix all the meats and chestnuts together in a 2-quart pie dish and pour over enough of the liquid to come no less than ¾ inch from the rim of the dish. Let cool.

3. Preheat the oven to 375°F. Roll out the pastry on a lightly floured work surface until it is slightly larger than the dish and use to cover the pie (see page 9). Trim any overhanging edges, then scallop with the back of a knife (see page 17). Lightly reroll the trimmings into leaf shapes and add these. Brush the pastry with beaten egg, make a hole in the center of the pie, and bake in the oven for 1 hour, until the pie crust is deep golden, covering the top with foil if the pastry begins to overbrown.

SUET CRUST VENISON PIE

SERVES 4

- 4 tablespoons all-purpose flour
- 4 tablespoons (½ stick) butter
- 2¾ lb venison stew meat, diced
- 1 tablespoon vegetable oil
- 7 oz bacon slices, chopped
- 1 onion, chopped
- 2 small leeks, chopped
- 4 garlic cloves, crushed
- 1 teaspoon juniper berries, crushed
- 1 cup beef or chicken stock
  2 cups red wine
- 3 tablespoons red currant jelly

- 4 tablespoons chopped parsley
- Salt and black pepper

Suet pastry
- 3¼ cups all-purpose flour, plus extra for dusting
- 1 teaspoon baking powder
- 1 teaspoon salt
- 1½ cups shredded suet or shortening
- 2 tablespoons grainy mustard
- ¾ cup water
- Beaten egg, to glaze

1. Preheat the oven to 325°F. Season the flour with salt and pepper and use to coat the venison. In a skillet, melt half the butter with the oil and brown the venison on all sides in batches, lifting the batches out with a slotted spoon into a casserole dish. Add the remaining butter to the skillet with the bacon, onion, and leeks and sauté until pale golden, about 10 minutes.

2. Tip in any flour left on the plate and add the garlic and juniper berries. Blend in the stock, wine, and red currant jelly and bring to a boil. Cook, stirring, for 2 minutes. Pour over the venison in the casserole, add the parsley, cover, and cook in the oven for 1½ hours, until the meat is tender.

3. Preheat the oven to 375°F. In a bowl, combine the flour, baking powder, salt, and suet. Stir the mustard into the water and add to the bowl. Mix to a firm dough, adding a dash more water if it is dry and crumbly. Knead on a floured work surface until smooth. Ladle the venison mixture into a pie dish with a slotted spoon and pour over enough of the liquid to come no less than ¾ inch from the rim of the dish. Roll out the pastry on a floured surface until it is larger than the dish and use to cover the pie (see page 9), then crimp the edges (see page 10). Brush with beaten egg, make a hole in the pie center, and bake in the oven for 45 minutes, or until golden.

ALL-IN-ONE CHICKEN PIE

SERVES 4

- ½ lb broccoli florets
- 1 tablespoon olive oil
- ¾ lb boneless, skinless chicken breasts, cubed
- 6 bacon slices, chopped
- 2 small carrots, chopped
- 2 tablespoons (¼ stick) butter
- 3 tablespoons all-purpose flour, plus extra for dusting
- 1¼ cups milk
- 1 tablespoon white wine vinegar
- 1 teaspoon Dijon mustard
- ¾ cup crème fraîche or thick sour cream
- 2 tablespoons chopped tarragon or parsley
- 1 lb store-bought pie crust (or use homemade Short-Crust Pastry—see page 14), chilled
- Beaten egg, to glaze

1. In a saucepan, cook the broccoli in boiling water until tender, 5 minutes. Drain and refresh with cold water, then set aside. In a nonstick skillet, heat the oil and sauté the chicken and bacon over medium heat for 7–8 minutes. Add the carrots and cook until golden all over, 3–4 minutes. Remove from the heat.

2. In a saucepan, melt the butter and add the flour. Cook gently, stirring, for 1 minute, then remove from the heat and gradually blend in the milk. Add the vinegar and mustard and mix well. Return to the heat and cook, stirring continuously, until bubbling and thickened. Stir in the crème fraîche or sour cream and herbs. Add the chicken and vegetables and stir well to coat, then transfer to a pie dish. Let cool.

3. Preheat the oven to 350°F. Roll out the pie crust or pastry on a lightly floured work surface until it is slightly larger than the dish and use to cover the pie (see page 9), then decorate with any remaining pastry trimmings, if liked (see page 11). Brush with beaten egg, make a hole in the center of the pie, and bake in the oven for 25–30 minutes, until the pie crust is crisp and golden.

CHICKEN &
HAM PIE

SERVES 5

- 1 chicken, about 3¼ lb
- 1 onion, peeled and halved
- 1 teaspoon black peppercorns
- 3 bay leaves
- 2 tablespoons (¼ stick) butter
- 3 tablespoons all-purpose flour, plus extra for dusting
- 4 tablespoons crème fraiche or thick sour cream

- ⅓ cup finely chopped parsley
- 7-oz piece of fully cooked ham, cut into small chunks
- 1 lb puff pastry (see page 17 for homemade), thawed if frozen but chilled
- Beaten egg, to glaze
- Salt and black pepper

1. Rinse out the chicken and remove any trussing. Place in a pot in which it fits quite snugly. Add the onion, peppercorns, and bay leaves to the pot and just cover with cold water. Bring to a boil, then reduce the heat to its lowest setting, cover, and cook until the chicken feels tender when pierced with a skewer, about 1 hour. Let cool in the liquid.

2. Lift the chicken from the stock and measure 1¾ cups of the stock into a measuring cup. (Chill or freeze the remaining stock for another time.) In a saucepan, melt the butter and add the flour. Cook gently, stirring, for 1 minute, then remove from the heat and gradually blend in the stock. Return to the heat and cook gently, stirring continuously, until bubbling and slightly thickened. Stir in the crème fraîche or sour cream and parsley, and season to taste with salt and pepper. Let cool.

3. Pull the chicken meat away from the bones, discarding the skin and bones. Chop all the meat into small pieces and place in a pie dish with the ham. Add the sauce and stir well to coat.

4. Preheat the oven to 400°F. Roll out the pastry on a lightly floured work surface until it is slightly larger than the dish and use to cover the pie (see page 9), then scallop the edges with the back of a knife (see page 17). Brush the pastry with beaten egg, make a hole in the center of the pie, and bake in the oven for about 40 minutes, until the pie crust is deep golden.

PORK PIE WITH TARRAGON & PRUNES

SERVES 6

- 2 tablespoons all-purpose flour, plus extra for dusting
- 2 lb pork shoulder blade steak, diced
- 2 tablespoons (¼ stick) butter
- 1 tablespoon vegetable oil
- 2 onions, chopped
- 3 celery stalks, thinly sliced
- 1 cup pork or chicken stock
- ⅔ cup dry white wine
- Leaves from several large tarragon sprigs
- Scant 1 cup coarsely chopped pitted prunes
- 4 tablespoons crème fraîche or sour cream
- Double quantity Short-Crust Pastry (see page 14), chilled
- Beaten egg, to glaze
- Salt and black pepper

1. Preheat the oven to 325°F. Season the flour with salt and pepper and use to coat the pork. In a large saucepan or flameproof casserole, melt the butter with the oil and brown the pork on all sides in batches, lifting the batches out with a slotted spoon onto a plate. Add the onions and celery to the pan and gently sauté until softened and lightly browned, 6–8 minutes.

2. Tip in any flour left on the plate and blend in the stock and wine. Bring to a boil, then reduce the heat. Return the meat to the pan with the tarragon, cover, and simmer very gently until the meat is tender, about 1–1¼ hours. Remove from the heat and stir in the prunes and crème fraîche or sour cream. Season to taste and let cool, then turn into a pie dish.

3. Preheat the oven to 400°F. Roll out the pastry on a lightly floured work surface until it is slightly larger than the dish and use to cover the pie (see page 9), then scallop the edges with the back of a knife (see page 17). Brush the pastry with beaten egg, make a hole in the center of the pie, and bake in the oven for 30–40 minutes, until the pie crust is deep golden.

RAISED PICNIC PIE

SERVES 10

- 1 lb pork sausage meat
- 1 lb lean diced pork
- 1 teaspoon cumin seed, lightly crushed
- 2 shallots, finely chopped
- Single quantity Hot Water Crust Pastry (see page 21), chilled
- All-purpose flour, for dusting
- Beaten egg, to glaze
- 2 sheets of gelatin
- 1¼ cups pork or chicken stock
- Salt and black pepper

1. Preheat the oven to 400°F. In a bowl, mix together the sausage meat, pork, cumin, shallots, and plenty of salt and pepper. (This is easiest done with your hands.) Roll out a generous two-thirds of the pastry on a floured work surface into a 12-inch circle and use to line a 7-inch loose-bottom cake pan about 3 inches deep, letting it extend slightly over the top edges. Line with wax paper and half-fill with dry beans or rice or pie weights. Blind bake in the oven for 25 minutes (see page 9). Lift out the paper and beans.

2. Pile the meat mixture into the pie shell, doming it up in the center. Brush the top edges of the cooked pastry with beaten egg. Roll out the remaining pastry until it is slightly larger than the pan and position on top (see page 9). Press the pastry edges together firmly to seal and trim off the excess, then use the trimmings to decorate with pastry leaves, if liked (see page 11). Brush the pastry with beaten egg, make a hole in the center of the pie, and bake in the oven for 30 minutes. Reduce the oven temperature to 350°F and bake for another hour. Carefully remove the pie from the pan and place on a cookie sheet. Brush the sides of the pie with beaten egg and bake for an additional 30 minutes. Let cool.

3. In a bowl of cold water, let the gelatin sheets soak for 5 minutes. In a saucepan, bring the stock to a boil. Drain the gelatin and lower into the stock, stirring briefly to dissolve. Let cool but not set. Position a small funnel over the hole in the center of pie and slowly pour in the stock until the pie is filled. Chill for several hours before serving.

CRUMBLE-TOPPED FISH PIE

SERVES 4

- 6 oz store-bought pie crust (or use homemade Short-Crust Pastry—see page 14), chilled
- 7 oz skinless cod fillet
- 7 oz skinless undyed finnan haddie (smoked haddock fillet)
- 1 cup milk
- 1 bay leaf
- 5 scallions, chopped
- 7 oz raw peeled shrimp
- ⅓ cup heavy cream

- 3 tablespoons all-purpose flour, plus extra for dusting
- 2 tablespoons (¼ stick) butter
- 3 tablespoons chopped parsley
- Salt and black pepper

Crumble topping
- 2 tablespoons (¼ stick) butter
- Heaping 2 cups coarse fresh white bread crumbs
- 3 tablespoons chopped parsley

1. Roll out the pie crust on a lightly floured work surface and use to line an 8-inch tart pan. Chill the pie shell for 30 minutes. Preheat the oven to 400°F. Line the pie shell with wax paper and half-fill with dry beans or rice or pie weights. Blind bake in the oven for 15 minutes (see page 9). Lift out the paper and beans and bake for another 5 minutes.

2. In a sauté pan, combine the fish, milk, and bay leaf and bring to a gentle boil. Simmer for 3 minutes, then remove from the heat, cover, and let cool for a few minutes. Strain the liquid into a pitcher, discard the bay leaf, and set aside. Flake the fish into large pieces and place in the pie shell with the scallions and shrimp.

3. In a saucepan, combine the reserved milk with the cream, flour, and butter. Stir continuously over low heat until the butter has melted. Continue to stir until the sauce thickens and reaches boiling point. Let simmer for 2–3 minutes, then remove from the heat and stir in the parsley. Season well with salt and pepper and pour over the fish.

4. Make the topping. In a skillet, melt the butter and gently pan-fry the bread crumbs until pale golden, 2–3 minutes. Stir in the parsley and spoon over the top of the pie. Bake in the oven for 20 minutes, until the top is golden and the sauce bubbles around the sides. Let cool before serving.

GARLICKY MUSSEL & POTATO PIE

SERVES 4-5

- 2 x 2-lb bags fresh mussels
- 4 tablespoons (½ stick) butter
- 2 onions, chopped
- 4 garlic cloves, crushed
- 3 tablespoons all-purpose flour, plus extra for dusting
- ¾ cup dry white wine
- 1¼ cups fish stock

- 1½ lb potatoes, peeled and cut into small chunks
- 6 tablespoons light cream
- 5 tablespoons chopped curly parsley
- 1 lb puff pastry (see page 17 for homemade), thawed if frozen but chilled
- Beaten egg, to glaze
- Salt and black pepper

1. Wash the mussels in cold water. Scrape off any barnacles and pull away the beards. Discard any with damaged shells or that don't open when tapped firmly with a knife.

2. In a large saucepan, melt the butter and gently sauté the onions for 5 minutes, adding the garlic toward the end of cooking. Add the flour and cook gently, stirring, for 1 minute. Remove from the heat and gradually blend in the wine, then the stock. Return to the heat and cook gently, stirring continuously, until bubbling and slightly thickened.

3. Tip in the mussels, cover, and cook, shaking the pan frequently, until the mussels have opened, about 5 minutes. Drain the mussels to a large bowl with a slotted spoon. Add the potatoes to the sauce in the pan, cover, and cook gently until the potatoes are just tender, 15 minutes. Stir in the cream and parsley, and season with salt and pepper. Remove the mussels from their shells, discarding any that have not opened, and return to the pan with any cooking juices in the bowl. Turn into a pie dish. Let cool.

4. Preheat the oven to 400°F. Roll out the pastry on a lightly floured work surface until it is slightly larger than the dish and use to cover the pie (see page 9), then scallop the edges with the back of a knife (see page 17). Brush the pastry with beaten egg, make a hole in the center of the pie, and bake in the oven for about 40 minutes, until the pie crust is deep golden.

HERBY COD & EGG PIE

SERVES 4
- 1¼ lb skinless cod, haddock, or pollock fillets
- ¾ cup milk
- 7 oz raw peeled shrimp
- 4 large soft-boiled eggs, shelled
- ⅔ cup (1 stick plus 2½ tablespoons) butter
- 1½ cups all-purpose flour, plus 3 tablespoons
- ⅔ cup light cream
- 4 tablespoons chopped parsley or dill weed
- Salt and black pepper

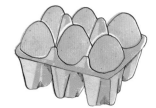

1. Preheat the oven to 375°F. In a skillet, combine the fish with the milk and some salt and pepper. Bring to a simmer, cover, and cook gently until the fish has turned opaque, about 5 minutes. Drain, reserving the liquid, and place the fish in a shallow ovenproof dish or pie dish, breaking it up into large pieces. Add the shrimp and eggs to the dish, pushing them down between the pieces of fish.

2. In a saucepan, melt 4 tablespoons (½ stick) of the butter. Add the 3 tablespoons flour and cook, stirring, for 1 minute. Remove from the heat and gradually blend in the reserved milk and the cream. Return to the heat and cook gently, stirring continuously, until bubbling and thickened. Stir in the parsley or dill weed and salt and pepper to taste, and pour over the filling.

3. Sift the remaining flour into a bowl or food processor. Add the remaining butter and cut in with a pastry blender or the fingertips or pulse with the food processor until the mixture resembles fine bread crumbs. Season lightly with salt and pepper and spoon over the filling. Bake the pie in the oven for about 40 minutes, until the crumble is golden.

SALMON IN PUFF PASTRY

SERVES 6-8

- 2 lb whole salmon, skinned and filleted
- 2 tablespoons (¼ stick) butter, plus extra for greasing
- 2 bacon slices, chopped
- 1¾ cups chopped white mushrooms
- ½ cup soft cheese with garlic and herbs

- 2 tablespoons milk
- 1 lb puff pastry (see page 17 for homemade), thawed if frozen but chilled
- All-purpose flour, for dusting
- Beaten egg, to glaze
- Salt and black pepper

1. Preheat the oven to 400°F. Grease a cookie sheet. Season the two salmon fillets with salt and pepper on both sides. In a skillet, melt the butter, add the bacon, and pan-fry until crisp, about 5 minutes. Add the mushrooms and sauté, stirring, until softened, about 2 minutes. Stir in the soft cheese and milk, and season to taste with salt and pepper. Cook gently, stirring, until well mixed. Remove from the heat and let cool.

2. Roll out half the pastry on a lightly floured work surface until 1 inch larger all round than the reassembled salmon fillets. Transfer to the cookie sheet and place one salmon fillet, skinned-side down, in the center. Spread with the cheese mixture and cover with the second salmon fillet, skinned-side up.

3. Brush the edges of the pastry with a little of the beaten egg. Roll out the remaining pastry and cover the fish. Trim the edges, then pinch them together to seal. Brush the pastry with beaten egg and arrange strips over the top. Bake in the oven for 35–40 minutes, until the pastry is crisp and deep golden.

SALMON, SHRIMP & SPINACH PIE

- -

SERVES 6

- 1½ lb chilled puff pastry (see page 17 for homemade), thawed if frozen but chilled
- Beaten egg, to glaze

Filling
- 2 tablespoons (¼ stick) butter
- 2 shallots, finely chopped
- Grated zest of 1 lemon

- 2 tablespoons all-purpose flour, plus extra for dusting
- 1¼ cups light cream
- ½ teaspoon grated nutmeg
- ½ lb frozen leaf spinach, thawed
- 1 lb skinless salmon fillet, cubed
- ½ lb raw peeled shrimp
- 1 tablespoon chopped tarragon
- Salt and black pepper

1. Roll out half the pastry on a lightly floured work surface to a 10-inch x 14-inch rectangle. Repeat with the remaining pastry. Cover with clean dish towels and let rest.

2. Make the filling. In a saucepan, melt the butter and gently sauté the shallots and lemon zest for 3 minutes. Add the flour and cook gently, stirring, for 1 minute. Remove from the heat and gradually blend in the cream. Return to the heat and cook gently, stirring continuously, until thickened. Remove from the heat and season with the nutmeg and salt and pepper. Cover closely with plastic wrap and let cool.

3. Preheat the oven to 425°F and put in a cookie sheet to heat. Line a large cookie sheet with parchment paper. Drain the spinach well and season lightly with salt and pepper. Lay one piece of pastry on the cookie sheet and spread the spinach over the top, leaving a 1-inch border at each end and a 2-inch border each side.

4. Stir the salmon, shrimp, and tarragon into the cooled cream mixture and spoon over the spinach. Brush the edges of the pastry with water and top with the other piece of pastry, pressing the edges together firmly to seal. Trim to neaten. "Scallop" the pastry edges (see page 17), then crimp (see page 10). Brush the pastry with beaten egg, make a hole in the top, and bake on the heated cookie sheet for 20 minutes. Reduce the temperature to 375°F and bake for 15 minutes, until the pastry is risen and golden.

CREAMY MUSHROOM & BLUE CHEESE PIES

MAKES 8
- 2 tablespoons (¼ stick) butter
- 1 tablespoon olive oil
- 1 onion, finely chopped
- ½ lb mixed mushrooms, sliced
- 2 garlic cloves, finely chopped
- 3 thyme sprigs, leaves torn from stems, plus extra (optional) for sprinkling
- 1 lb puff pastry (see page 17 for homemade), thawed if frozen but chilled
- All-purpose flour, for dusting
- ½ cup crème fraîche or thick sour cream
- 6 oz blue cheese, rind removed and diced
- Beaten egg, to glaze
- Sea salt and black pepper

1. Preheat the oven to 400°F. In a skillet, melt the butter with the oil and sauté the onion until just beginning to soften. Add the mushrooms and garlic and sauté, stirring, until golden. Remove from the heat, add the thyme leaves, and let cool.

2. Roll out the pastry thinly on a lightly floured work surface and trim to a 14-inch square, then cut into 16 squares. Spoon the mushroom mixture over the center of eight of the squares, then top with the crème fraîche or sour cream and blue cheese. Brush the edges of the filled squares with beaten egg, then cover each with a remaining pastry square.

3. Press the edges of the pastry together firmly to seal, then crimp, if liked (see page 10). Transfer to a cookie sheet. Slash the tops with a knife, brush with beaten egg, and sprinkle with sea salt and extra thyme, if liked. Bake in the oven for 20 minutes, until well risen and golden brown. Serve warm with salad, if liked.

ONION, THYME & POTATO PUFF

SERVES 6

- ½ lb new potatoes, peeled and very thinly sliced
- 3 tablespoons olive oil, plus extra for oiling
- 14 oz red onions, thinly sliced
- 1 tablespoon chopped thyme, plus extra sprigs for sprinkling
- 2 tablespoons balsamic vinegar
- 1 lb puff pastry (see page 17 for homemade), thawed if frozen but chilled
- All-purpose flour, for dusting
- 3½ oz Camembert or Brie
- Beaten egg, to glaze
- Sea salt and black pepper

1. In a saucepan, cook the potatoes in lightly salted boiling water until softened, 5 minutes. Drain and let cool. In a large skillet, heat the oil and sauté the onions very gently, stirring frequently, until soft and lightly browned, about 15 minutes. Stir in the chopped thyme, vinegar, and some black pepper, then let cool.

2. Preheat the oven to 425°F. Brush a cookie sheet with oil. Roll out half the pastry on a lightly floured work surface and cut out a 10-inch circle by cutting around an upturned bowl or plate. Place on the cookie sheet and brush the edges with beaten egg. Spread half the onion mixture over the pastry, keeping it ¾ inch away from the edges. Arrange a thin layer of potatoes on top and spread with the remaining onions. Slice the cheese over the onions.

3. Roll out the remaining pastry and cut out another circle in the same way. Position on top, pressing the pastry edges together firmly, then crimp the edges (see page 10). Brush the pastry with beaten egg and score shallow cuts, ¾ inch apart, across the top, first in one direction and then the other. Sprinkle with sea salt. Bake in the oven for 30 minutes, until well risen and deep golden. Serve warm or cold, scattered with extra thyme sprigs.

GLUTEN-FREE CHEESY PICNIC PIES

- -

MAKES 4

- 1 tablespoon olive oil, plus extra for oiling
- 1 onion, chopped
- 2 garlic cloves, finely chopped
- 1 zucchini, diced
- 1 yellow bell pepper, seeded and diced
- 1 red bell pepper, seeded and diced
- 14½-oz can diced tomatoes
- 1 tablespoon chopped rosemary or basil
- 1 teaspoon sugar
- Salt and black pepper

Pastry

- 1⅓ cups plus 1 tablespoon gluten-free bread flour
- ⅓ cup (½ stick plus 1⅓ tablespoons) butter, diced
- ½ cup diced sharp cheddar cheese, plus extra, shredded, for sprinkling
- 2 large egg yolks
- 2 teaspoons ice water
- Beaten egg, to glaze

1. In a saucepan, heat the oil and sauté the onion until softened, 5 minutes. Add the garlic, zucchini, and bell peppers and sauté briefly, then add the tomatoes, herbs, and sugar and season lightly with salt and pepper. Simmer, uncovered, until thickened, 10 minutes, stirring. Let cool.

2. Preheat the oven to 375°F. Brush a cookie sheet with oil. Make the pastry. Sift the flour into a bowl or food processor and season with salt and pepper. Add the butter and cut in with a pastry blender or the fingertips or pulse with the food processor until the mixture resembles fine bread crumbs. Mix in the diced cheddar, then add the egg yolks and enough ice water to mix or pulse to a firm dough.

3. Knead the dough briefly on a lightly floured work surface, then divide into four pieces. Roll out one piece between two sheets of plastic wrap into a 7-inch circle. Remove the top sheet of plastic wrap and spoon a quarter of the filling in the center. Brush the pastry edges with beaten egg, then fold the pastry circle in half. Peel off the plastic wrap and lift onto the cookie sheet. Press the edges together to seal and press together any breaks in the pastry. Repeat with the remaining pastry pieces and filling.

4. Brush the pies with beaten egg, sprinkle with the cheddar, and bake in the oven for 20 minutes, until the pie crust is golden brown. Let cool.

GOLDEN MUSHROOM & LEEK PIES

MAKES 4

- 2 tablespoons (¼ stick) butter
- 2 leeks, thinly sliced
- 1 lb crimini or button mushrooms, quartered
- 1 tablespoon all-purpose flour
- 1 cup milk
- ⅔ cup heavy cream
- Scant 1 cup shredded sharp cheddar cheese
- 4 tablespoons finely chopped parsley
- 2 sheets of store-bought rolled puff pastry, thawed if frozen but chilled
- Beaten egg, to glaze

1. In a large saucepan, melt the butter and sauté the leeks for 1–2 minutes. Add the mushrooms and sauté for 2 minutes. Add the flour and cook gently, stirring, for 1 minute. Remove from the heat and gradually blend in the milk and cream. Return to the heat and cook gently, stirring continuously, until bubbling and thickened. Stir in the cheddar and parsley and cook, stirring, for 1–2 minutes. Remove from the heat and let cool.

2. Preheat the oven to 425°F. Divide the mushroom mixture between four individual pie dishes. Cut four circles from the pastry sheets large enough to cover the dishes. Brush the rims of the dishes with beaten egg, position the pastry circles on top, and press the edges down firmly, then press a fork around the edges to decorate. Brush the pastry with beaten egg, cut a couple of slits in the top of each pie, and bake in the oven for 15–20 minutes, until the pie crust is golden brown. Serve right away.

TIP

- For curried ham & mushroom pies, after cooking the mushrooms, add 1 teaspoon medium curry powder and ½ teaspoon turmeric and cook, stirring, for 1 minute, before adding the flour and continuing with the recipe. Once the sauce has thickened, stir in 1½ cups diced cooked ham in place of the cheese and 4 tablespoons chopped cilantro leaves instead of the parsley. Make and bake the pies as above.

GREEK TOMATO & FETA PIE

SERVES 4

- 3 green bell peppers, seeded and cut into chunks
- 2 small red onions, sliced
- ½ cup olive oil
- 2 garlic cloves, crushed
- 2 cups cherry tomatoes, halved
- ½ teaspoon dried oregano
- ¼ cup sun-dried tomatoes in oil, drained and thinly sliced
- 1⅓ cups crumbled feta cheese
- 3 sheets of phyllo dough, thawed if frozen but chilled
- Clear honey, for drizzling (optional)
- 1½ teaspoons sesame seed, lightly toasted
- Salt and black pepper

1. Preheat the oven to 375°F. Scatter the bell peppers and onions into a shallow ovenproof dish. Mix 2 tablespoons of the oil with the garlic and drizzle over the vegetables. Toss the ingredients together, season with salt and pepper, and bake in the oven for 40 minutes, until the vegetables are soft and lightly colored.

2. Scatter in the cherry tomatoes, oregano, sun-dried tomatoes, and feta, season lightly with salt and pepper, and mix the ingredients together. Drizzle with all but 2 tablespoons of the remaining oil.

3. Place one sheet of phyllo dough over the filling, crumpling the pastry so it's not completely flat. Brush with oil and sprinkle with ½ teaspoon of the sesame seed. Add a second layer of pastry, brush with the remaining oil, and sprinkle with another ½ teaspoon sesame seed. Arrange the third layer of pastry over the pie, drizzle with the honey and scatter with the remaining sesame seed and a bit of pepper. Bake in the oven for 35 minutes, until the pastry is golden.

MINI VEGETABLE PIES

MAKES 6

- ¾ lb store-bought pie crust (or use homemade Short-Crust Pastry—see page 14)
- All-purpose flour, for dusting
- ¾ lb puff pastry dough (see page 17 for homemade), thawed if frozen but chilled
- Beaten egg, to glaze

Filling
- 4 tablespoons extra virgin olive oil
- 1 lb button mushrooms, quartered
- 1 onion, finely chopped
- 2 garlic cloves, crushed
- 1 tablespoon chopped thyme
- ½ lb carrots, peeled and chopped
- ½ lb parsnips, peeled and chopped
- ⅔ cup red wine
- 2 cups strained tomatoes
- Salt and black pepper

1. Make the filling. In a flameproof casserole, heat half the oil and sauté the mushrooms seasoned with salt and pepper until golden, 4–5 minutes. Remove with a slotted spoon and set aside. Add the remaining oil to the pan and sauté the onion, garlic, and thyme for 5 minutes. Add the carrots and parsnips and cook until softened and lightly golden, 5 minutes.

2. Add the wine to the pan and boil rapidly for 3 minutes, then stir in the strained tomatoes, mushrooms, and more salt and pepper. Bring to a boil, cover, and simmer for 20 minutes. Remove the lid and cook until the vegetables are tender and the sauce is really thick, about 20 minutes. Cool.

3. Preheat the oven to 425°F. Divide the pie crust into six pieces, roll out each piece on a lightly floured work surface, and use to line six individual 5-inch pie dishes, letting the pastry extend slightly over the top edges. Divide the puff pastry into six pieces and roll out each piece thinly until slightly larger than the dishes.

4. Fill the pie shells with the cooled vegetable stew. Brush the top edges of the pie shells with beaten egg and position the puff pastry on top, pressing the edges together firmly to seal. Trim the excess pastry. Brush the tops with beaten egg, cut a small slit in the center of each pie, and bake in the oven for 25 minutes, until the pie crust is golden. Serve hot.

SPINACH & FETA PIE WITH PINE NUTS

- -

SERVES 4-6

- 1½ lb fresh spinach leaves, washed
- 1⅔ cups crumbled feta cheese
- ½ teaspoon crushed red pepper
- ¾ cup freshly grated Parmesan cheese
- ⅓ cup pine nuts, toasted
- 4 tablespoons chopped dill weed
- 3 tablespoons chopped tarragon

- 3 large eggs, lightly beaten
- 1 teaspoon grated nutmeg
- ½ lb phyllo dough, thawed if frozen but chilled
- 5–8 tablespoons olive oil, plus extra for oiling
- 1 tablespoon sesame seed
- Salt and black pepper

1. In a large saucepan, gently cook the spinach just with the water clinging to the leaves until wilted and soft. Drain, then squeeze out excess water.

2. In a bowl, combine the feta with the spinach, red pepper, Parmesan, pine nuts, and herbs. Add the beaten eggs with plenty of salt and pepper and the grated nutmeg, and mix well.

3. Preheat the oven to 375°F. Brush an 8-inch loose-bottom cake pan with oil. Working quickly, brush the top sheet of phyllo lightly with oil. (Keep the remaining sheets of phyllo dough covered with a clean dish towel to prevent drying out.) Lay the sheet in the bottom of the pan with the edges overlapping the rim. Brush the next sheet of phyllo and lay it in the opposite direction from the first sheet to completely cover the bottom of the pan. Repeat this process until you have a pie shell of six to eight sheets of phyllo and there are at least three sheets of phyllo remaining for a lid.

4. Spoon the spinach mixture into the phyllo shell, pushing it in well with the back of the spoon and leveling the surface. Brush the next sheet of phyllo with oil and then cut the length of the remaining stack of phyllo into 2-inch wide strips. One by one, place the strips over the top of the spinach in a casual folded arrangement, remembering to brush all of them with oil. Fold in the overhanging phyllo toward the center of the pie. Sprinkle with the sesame seed and bake in the oven for 1 hour. Let cool for 15 minutes, then gently push the pie up and out of the pan. Serve warm or cold.

CHILIED PUMPKIN & TOMATO PIES

MAKES 4

- 1 tablespoon olive oil, plus extra for oiling
- 1 large red onion, chopped
- 14 oz seeded pumpkin or butternut squash, peeled and cut into small dice
- 2 garlic cloves, finely chopped
- ½ teaspoon smoked paprika

- 14½-oz can diced tomatoes
- Single quantity Short-Crust Pastry (see page 14), chilled
- All-purpose flour, for dusting
- ⅔ cup crumbled feta cheese
- Beaten egg, to glaze
- Salt and black pepper

1. In a saucepan, heat the oil and sauté the onion and pumpkin or squash until softened, about 5 minutes. Stir in the garlic and paprika, then the tomatoes and salt and pepper to taste. Cover and simmer until the pumpkin or squash is just tender, 15 minutes, stirring occasionally. Let cool.

2. Preheat the oven to 350°F. Lightly brush four individual 5-inch fluted loose-bottom tart pans with oil. Divide the pastry into four pieces, then roll out each piece on a lightly floured work surface and use to line the pans, letting the pastry extend slightly over the top edges, reserving the trimmings.

3. Stand the pans on a cookie sheet, spoon in the cooled filling, then scatter with the feta. Brush the top edges of the pie shells with beaten egg. Roll out the pastry trimmings and cut into narrow strips, long enough to go over the tops of the pies. Arrange as a lattice on each pie (see page 10), then brush with beaten egg. Bake in the oven for 20–25 minutes, until golden brown. Let stand for 5 minutes, then remove from the pans and serve warm or cold.

TIP

- For chilied pumpkin & bacon pies, make up the filling and pie shells as above, omitting the feta and adding 4 broiled and diced Canadian bacon slices to the filling. Add the pastry lattice and bake as above.

DEEP DISH PUFF APPLE PIE P98

SWEET PIES

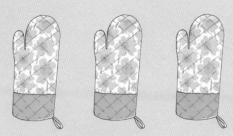

RUSTIC MARZIPAN & APRICOT PIE

SERVES 6-8

- Butter, for greasing
- 1 lb apricots
- 3 tablespoons superfine sugar
- ½ teaspoon ground cinnamon
- 1 lb puff pastry (see page 17 for homemade), thawed if frozen but chilled

- All-purpose flour, for dusting
- ½ lb marzipan
- Beaten egg, to glaze
- Vanilla Sugar (see page 25), for dusting

1. Preheat the oven to 400°F. Grease a large cookie sheet. Quarter the apricots, discarding the pits. In a bowl, toss the apricots with the superfine sugar and cinnamon.

2. Roll out the pastry on a lightly floured work surface into a roughly shaped 18-inch circle. Transfer the pastry to the cookie sheet. Lightly knead the marzipan into a ball and roll out into a 10-inch circle. Position on the center of the pastry.

3. Tip the apricots out onto the marzipan and spread out almost to the edges. Bring the edges of the pastry up over the filling, folding it to fit and pressing the folds together very firmly so they don't burst open during baking. Brush the pastry with beaten egg. Bake in the oven for 40 minutes, until the pie crust is risen and deep golden. Dust with plenty of vanilla sugar and slide onto a plate. Serve with pouring cream.

PLUM & GINGER PIE

SERVES 6

- 2 lb ripe juicy plums
- ½ cup raw brown sugar, plus extra for sprinkling
- ½ teaspoon apple pie spice
- 1 tablespoon lemon juice
- 4 tablespoons (½ stick) butter

Pastry
- 2 cups all-purpose flour, plus extra for dusting

- ⅔ cup (1 stick plus 2½ tablespoons) slightly salted butter in one piece, chilled until almost frozen
- 4 balls preserved ginger, from a jar
- 2 large egg yolks
- About 6 tablespoons ice water
- Beaten egg, to glaze

1. Make the pastry. Sift the flour into a bowl. Holding the butter with cool fingertips or by its folded-back wrapper, shred it directly over the flour, stirring it into the flour frequently so it doesn't clump together. Finely grate in the ginger. Add the egg yolks and stir in enough of the ice water with a palette knife to make a firm dough. Use your hands to bring the dough together. It should be firm, but not so dry that it doesn't cling together, so add a dash more water if necessary.

2. Knead the dough briefly on a lightly floured work surface into a ball. Wrap in foil and chill for at least 1 hour before using.

3. Halve the plums, discarding the pits, and scatter in a pie dish with the sugar and spice. Drizzle with the lemon juice and dot with the butter. Roll out the pastry on a lightly floured work surface until it is slightly larger than the dish and use to cover the pie (see page 9), then press a fork around the edges to decorate. Brush the pastry with beaten egg, make a hole in the center of the pie, and bake in the oven for about 40 minutes, until the pie crust is deep golden. Serve warm with Vanilla Sabayon (see page 25) or pouring cream.

LINZERTORTE

This delicious pie takes its name from the Austrian town of Linz. It is distinguished by the pastry, which is made with ground almonds.

SERVES 6

- 1¼ cups all-purpose flour, plus extra for dusting
- ½ teaspoon ground cinnamon
- ⅓ cup (1½ stick plus 1⅓ tablespoons) butter, plus extra for greasing
- ¼ cup superfine sugar
- ½ cup ground almonds
- 2 teaspoons finely grated lemon zest
- 2 extra-large egg yolks
- About 1 tablespoon lemon juice
- 1 cup raspberry jam
- Sifted confectioners' sugar, for dusting

1. Preheat the oven to 375°F. Grease a 7–8-inch fluted flan ring placed on a cookie sheet. Sift the flour and cinnamon into a bowl or food processor. Add the butter and cut in with a pastry blender or the fingertips or pulse with the food processor until the mixture resembles fine bread crumbs. Mix in the sugar, ground almonds, and lemon zest, then add the egg yolks and enough lemon juice to mix or pulse to a firm dough.

2. Knead the dough briefly on a lightly floured work surface. Roll out two-thirds of the dough and use to line the flan ring. Fill the pie shell with the raspberry jam. Roll out the remaining dough with any trimmings thinly, cut into strips, and use to create a lattice top for the pie (see page 10).

3. Bake in the oven for 25–30 minutes, until the pastry is golden brown. Let cool, then remove the flan ring. Dust the top with sifted confectioners' sugar just before serving.

SPICED PEAR CRUMBLE PIE

SERVES 6

- 1 cup all-purpose flour, plus extra for dusting
- 1 cup self-rising whole-wheat flour
- 1 teaspoon apple pie spice
- ½ cup plus 1 tablespoon (1 stick plus 1 tablespoon) butter, chilled and diced
- ¼ cup light brown sugar
- About 2 tablespoons ice water
- 2 large ripe pears
- 1 cup crème fraîche or thick sour cream
- 2 large eggs, lightly beaten
- 1 tablespoon superfine sugar

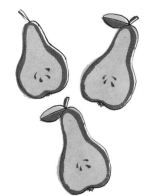

1. Sift the flours and spice into a bowl or food processor. Add the butter and cut in with a pastry blender or the fingertips or pulse with the food processor until the mixture resembles fine bread crumbs. For the crumble, transfer about a quarter of the mixture to a separate bowl and stir in the brown sugar. Set aside.

2. Add enough ice water to the unsweetened mixture to mix or pulse to a firm dough. Knead briefly on a lightly floured surface, then roll out and use to line an 8-inch tart pan or pie plate. Chill for 20 minutes (see page 9). Preheat the oven to 400°F.

3. Line the pie shell with wax paper and half-fill with dry beans or rice or pie weights. Blind bake in the oven for 20 minutes (see page 9). Lift out the paper and beans. Reduce the oven to 350°F.

4. Peel and core the pears, then cut the flesh into small dice. Spread evenly over the pie shell. In a bowl, beat together the crème fraîche or sour cream, eggs, and superfine sugar, then pour evenly over the top. Sprinkle with the reserved crumble and bake for 45–50 minutes, until the topping is crisp and golden brown. Serve warm or cold.

BLUEBERRY PIE

Fresh blueberries have a fairly short season, but frozen berries are available and can be used equally successfully in this pie. The flavor of this attractive fruit is intensified by cooking.

SERVES 6

- Single quantity Pâte Sucrée (see page 16), chilled
- All-purpose flour, for dusting
- 1⅔ cups fresh or frozen blueberries, thawed if frozen
- 2 tablespoons sugar
- Milk, to glaze
- ½ cup slivered almonds

1. Roll out about two-thirds of the pastry thinly on a lightly floured work surface and use to line an 8-inch tart pan. Chill for 30 minutes. Preheat the oven to 375°F.

2. Spread the blueberries evenly over the pie shell and sprinkle with the sugar. Roll out the remaining pastry with any trimmings thinly, cut into strips, and use to create a lattice top for the pie (see page 10). Brush the pastry with milk and sprinkle the slivered almonds over the surface.

3. Bake in the oven for 30–35 minutes, until the pastry is golden and the blueberries are tender. Serve warm or cold with cream or crème fraîche.

HONEYED PECAN PIE

SERVES 8

- Single quantity Pâte Sucrée (see page 16), chilled
- All-purpose flour, for dusting
- Scant ⅔ cup clear honey
- 1 cup light brown sugar
- ⅓ cup (½ stick plus 1⅓ tablespoons) butter, plus extra for greasing
- ¼ teaspoon ground cinnamon
- 1 teaspoon vanilla extract
- 3 large eggs
- 1½ cups pecans

1. Grease a 9-inch fluted loose-bottom tart pan 1 inch deep. Roll out the pastry thinly on a lightly floured work surface and use to line the pan. Trim the excess pastry with kitchen shears so it stands a bit above the top of the pan. Prick the bottom with a fork, then chill the pie shell for 15 minutes. Preheat the oven to 350°F.

2. Line the pie shell with wax paper and half-fill with dry beans or rice or pie weights. Blind bake in the oven for 10 minutes (see page 9). Lift out the paper and beans and bake for another 5 minutes. Remove from the oven and reduce the temperature to 350°F.

3. Meanwhile, in a saucepan, combine the honey, sugar, butter, and cinnamon and heat gently, stirring occasionally, until melted. Let cool slightly. In a pitcher, beat the vanilla extract with the eggs, then gradually beat into the cooled honey mixture. Pour into the pie shell and arrange the pecans over the top. Carefully transfer to the oven and bake for 25–30 minutes, until the filling is set and the nuts have darkened. Check after 15 minutes and cover the top loosely with foil if the top seems to be browning too quickly. Let cool in the pan for 30 minutes. Serve with scoops of vanilla ice cream, if liked.

SWEET CHERRY PIES

MAKES 4

- ⅔ cup superfine sugar, plus extra for sprinkling
- 1 tablespoon cornstarch
- ½ teaspoon ground star anise or cinnamon
- 1 lb frozen pitted black cherries, just thawed and halved
- Single quantity Pâte Sucrée (see page 16), flavored with grated orange zest, chilled
- All-purpose flour, for dusting
- Milk or beaten egg, to glaze

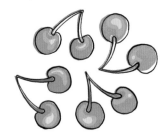

1. Preheat the oven to 350°F. In a bowl, mix the sugar, cornstarch, and spice together, then add the cherries and toss together. Roll out two-thirds of the pastry thinly on a lightly floured surface. Use to line four individual 4-inch fluted loose-bottom tart pans.

2. Spoon the cherry mixture into the pie shells. Roll out the remaining pastry with any trimmings and use a 4-inch fluted cookie cutter to cut out four circles. Brush the top edges of the pie shells with milk or beaten egg, position the pastry circles on top, and press the edges together firmly to seal. Slash the tops with a knife, then brush with milk or beaten egg and lightly sprinkle with sugar.

3. Bake the pies in the oven for 20–25 minutes, until the pie crust is golden. Let stand for 15 minutes, then loosen the edges of the pastry and remove the pies from the pans. Serve warm or cold with Crème Anglaise (see page 24) or Kirsch Custard (see Tip), if liked.

TIP

- For kirsch custard, to serve as an accompaniment, in a bowl, whip 3 large egg yolks with 3 tablespoons superfine sugar and 2 teaspoons cornstarch until smooth. In a saucepan, heat 1¼ cups milk just to boiling point, gradually beat into the yolks, and pour back into the pan. Slowly bring almost to a boil, stirring continuously, until thickened. Remove from the heat and stir in 2 tablespoons kirsch.

CRANBERRY & VANILLA PIE

SERVES 8

- 1 lb fresh or frozen cranberries
- 3 apples, peeled, cored, and coarsely chopped
- 4 tablespoons cranberry or other red fruit jelly
- ½ cup superfine sugar, plus extra for sprinkling
- 2 teaspoons cornstarch
- 1 tablespoon water
- 2 teaspoons vanilla bean paste or extract
- 1 lb puff pastry (see page 17 for homemade), thawed if frozen but chilled
- All-purpose flour, for dusting
- Beaten egg, to glaze

1. In a saucepan, combine the cranberries with the apples, jelly, and sugar. Heat gently until the jelly has dissolved and the cranberries are beginning to soften, about 5 minutes. Blend the cornstarch with the water to a paste and add to the pan. Cook, stirring, until thickened, 2–3 minutes. Remove from the heat, stir in the vanilla, and let cool.

2. Preheat the oven to 400°F. Roll out a generous half of the pastry on a lightly floured work surface and use to line an 8-inch loose-bottom layer cake pan about 1¾ inches deep, letting it extend slightly over the top edges. Spoon the filling into the center, spreading it to the edges. Brush the top edges of the pastry with beaten egg. Roll out the remaining pastry with any trimmings until it is slightly larger than the pan and position on top (see page 9). Press the pastry edges together firmly to seal and trim off the excess, then crimp the edges (see page 10) or press with a fork to decorate.

3. Brush the pie crust with beaten egg, make a hole in the center of the pie, and bake in the oven for 35 minutes, until risen and deep golden. Let stand for 20 minutes so that the juices thicken slightly, then carefully remove the pie from the pan and sprinkle with sugar. Serve with Crème Anglaise (see page 24) or ice cream.

PUMPKIN PIE

SERVES 6-8

- Single quantity Pâte Sucrée (see page 16), chilled
- All-purpose flour, for dusting
- I cup homemade pumpkin purée (see Tip) or 15-oz can pumpkin purée
- 2 large eggs, lightly beaten
- ⅔ cup light cream
- Heaping ⅓ cup superfine sugar
- I teaspoon ground cinnamon
- ½ teaspoon ground ginger
- ¼ teaspoon grated nutmeg

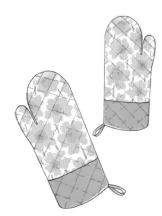

1. Preheat the oven to 375°F. Roll out the pastry on a lightly floured work surface and use to line a 9-inch pie dish. Reroll the trimmings thinly and cut into leaf shapes (see page 11). Brush the edge of the pie lightly with water and attach the leaves.

2. In a bowl, mix together the pumpkin purée, eggs, cream, sugar, and spices. Pour into the pie shell. Bake in the oven for 45–50 minutes, until the filling has set. Let cool. Serve with whipped cream.

TIP

- To make pumpkin purée, steam or boil chunks of peeled and seeded pumpkin until tender, 15–20 minutes, then drain thoroughly. Purée in a food processor or blender, or press them through a strainer.

CHERRY & ALMOND PITHIVIERS

- -

SERVES 8

- 15-oz can pitted cherries in light syrup
- 2 teaspoons cornstarch
- 4 tablespoons (½ stick) slightly salted butter, very soft, plus extra for greasing
- Heaping ⅓ cup superfine sugar, plus 1 teaspoon
- 2 large eggs, lightly beaten
- 1¼ cups ground almonds
- 1 teaspoon almond extract
- 1 lb puff pastry (see page 17 for homemade), thawed if frozen but chilled
- All-purpose flour, for dusting
- Beaten egg, for brushing
- 1 large egg yolk
- 1 teaspoon water
- 2 tablespoons slivered almonds
- Sifted confectioners' sugar, for dusting

1. Drain the cherries through a strainer, catching the juices in a bowl. Put 3 tablespoons of the juice in a saucepan and blend in the cornstarch. Pour in the remaining juice and cook gently until the juice is thickened and bubbling. Stir in the cherries and cook for another minute. Remove from the heat, tip into a bowl, and let cool.

2. Preheat the oven to 425°F. Grease a cookie sheet. In a bowl, beat the butter with the superfine sugar, eggs, ground almonds, and almond extract to make a thick, smooth paste. Roll out half the pastry on a lightly floured work surface and cut out an 11-inch circle by cutting around an upturned bowl or plate. Place on the cookie sheet and brush the edges with beaten egg. Spread the almond mixture over the pastry, keeping ¾ inch away from the edges. Spoon the cherry mixture on top.

3. Roll out the remaining pastry and cut out another circle in the same way. Position on top, pressing the pastry edges together firmly, then scallop the edges with the back of a knife (see page 17). Mix the egg yolk with the water and remaining 1 teaspoon superfine sugar. Brush over the top of the pastry. Sprinkle with the slivered almonds and bake in the oven for 30 minutes, until well risen and deep golden. Serve warm or cold, dusted with sifted confectioners' sugar.

BANOFFEE PIE

SERVES 6

- 5 oz rich tea biscuits or plain cookies
- 5 tablespoons (½ stick plus 1 tablespoon) butter
- 1 tablespoon dark corn syrup
- 1¼ cups heavy cream
- 2 bananas
- Juice of ½ lemon

Filling
- 7 tablespoons (½ stick plus 3 tablespoons) butter
- ½ cup dark brown sugar
- 14-oz can whole condensed milk

To decorate
- Diced toffees
- Grated chocolate (optional)

1. Crush the biscuits or cookies in a plastic bag with a rolling pin. In a saucepan, melt the butter with the syrup, then remove from the heat and stir in the crumbs. Tip into an 8-inch fluted loose-bottom tart pan, then press over the bottom and up the sides with the back of a spoon to create an even layer. Chill for 30 minutes.

2. Make the filling. In a clean, dry saucepan, melt the butter with the sugar, add the condensed milk, and stir well. Bring to a boil, then cook over medium heat, stirring continuously, until the mixture begins to thicken, smells of toffee, and crystallizes around the edges, 4–5 minutes. Be careful not to overheat as the milk can scorch easily. Pour the toffee into the pie shell, let cool, then chill for 3½–4½ hours, until ready to serve.

3. In a bowl, whip the cream until it forms soft swirls. Slice the bananas and toss with the lemon juice, then fold into the cream and spoon over the pie. Decorate the top with diced toffees and grated chocolate, if liked. Serve within 2 hours of decorating.

LEMON & PASSION FRUIT PIE

In this unusual pie, the tartness of the lemon tempers the mild sweetness of the yellow-fleshed passion fruit.

SERVES 8

- Single quantity Pâte Sucrée (see page 16), chilled
- All-purpose flour, for dusting
- 4 large eggs
- ¼ cup sugar
- ⅔ cup heavy cream

- Finely grated zest and juice of 3 lemons

To decorate
- Seeds from 3 passion fruit
- ⅔ cup heavy cream

1. Roll out the pastry on a lightly floured work surface and use to line an 8-inch fluted tart pan but without trimming the excess pastry. Chill for 30 minutes. Preheat the oven to 325°F. Trim the pie shell, then line with wax paper and half-fill with dry beans or rice or pie weights. Blind bake in the oven for 15 minutes (see page 9). Lift out the paper and beans and bake for another 5 minutes.

2. In a bowl, beat the eggs and sugar together, then stir in the cream and lemon zest and juice. Pour into the pastry shell, level the top, and bake in the oven for 25–30 minutes, until just set. Let cool.

3. In a bowl, whip the cream until just holding its shape. Stir the seeds of two of the passion fruit into the cream, then spoon over the pie. Sprinkle with the remaining seeds and serve within 1 hour.

LEMON MERINGUE PIE

- -

When whipping the egg whites, some cooks like to add a pinch of salt or a few drops of lemon juice to help the foam keep its shape.

SERVES 6

- Single quantity Pâte Sucrée (see page 16), chilled
- All-purpose flour, for dusting
- 3 tablespoons cornstarch
- ½ cup superfine sugar
- ⅔ cup water
- Grated zest of 2 lemons
- Juice of 1 lemon
- 2 tablespoons (¼ stick) butter
- 2 large egg yolks

Meringue
- 3 large egg whites
- ¾ cup plus 2 tablespoons superfine sugar

1. Roll out the pastry on a lightly floured work surface and use to line an 8-inch tart pan. Chill for 30 minutes. Preheat the oven to 325°F. Line the pie shell with wax paper and half-fill with dry beans or rice or pie weights. Blind bake in the oven for 15 minutes (see page 9). Lift out the paper and beans and bake for another 5 minutes.

2. In a saucepan, combine the cornstarch and sugar, then stir in the water and lemon zest and juice until well blended. Bring to a boil, stirring continuously, until the sauce is thickened and smooth. Remove from the heat and stir in the butter. Let cool slightly.

3. In a bowl, beat the egg yolks, then beat in 2 tablespoons of the sauce and return the mixture to the pan. Cook gently until the sauce has thickened more, then pour into the pie shell. Bake in the oven for 15 minutes, until the filling has set.

4. Make the meringue. In a clean, dry, grease-free bowl, whip the egg whites until stiff and dry. Beat in 1 tablespoon of the sugar, then fold in the rest with a large metal spoon. Spread over the filling so it is completely covered. Bake for 10 minutes, until the meringue is golden. Serve warm or cold.

DEEP DISH APPLE & BLACKBERRY PIE

Apples and blackberries combine in this timeless classic. You can use frozen blackberries when fresh ones are not available.

SERVES 4-6

- Sunflower oil, for oiling
- 1½ lb baking apples
- 2 cups blackberries
- 2–4 tablespoons superfine sugar, plus extra for sprinkling
- 2 tablespoons (¼ stick) unsalted butter, diced
- ½ teaspoon ground cinnamon

Pastry
- 1½ cups plus 2 tablespoons all-purpose flour
- ½ teaspoon salt
- ½ cup plus 1 tablespoon (1 stick plus 1 tablespoon) butter, chilled and diced
- 2 tablespoons ice water
- All-purpose flour, for dusting
- Milk, to glaze

1. Make the pastry. Sift the flour and salt into a bowl or food processor. Add the butter and cut in with a pastry blender or the fingertips or pulse with the food processor until the mixture resembles fine bread crumbs. Add enough of the ice water to mix or pulse to a firm dough. Knead the dough briefly on a lightly floured work surface, then form into a flat disk. Wrap in foil and chill for 20 minutes.

2. Preheat the oven to 400°F. Brush a 1-quart pie dish lightly with oil. Peel, core, and thickly slice the apples, then place in the pie dish. Add the blackberries, sugar, butter, and cinnamon, and stir well until evenly combined.

3. Roll out the pastry until it is slightly larger than the dish and use to cover the pie (see page 9). Brush the pastry with milk, make a hole in the center of the pie, and bake in the oven for 20 minutes. Reduce the temperature to 350°F and bake for another 15–20 minutes, until the pastry is crisp and golden. Sprinkle lightly with sugar before serving.

CHOCOLATE VELVET PIE

This chocolate shortbread crust is an interesting variation on traditional plain shortbread. Swirls of whipped heavy cream would make a decadent finishing touch.

SERVES 10

- 4 teaspoons powdered gelatin
- 3 tablespoons cold water
- ⅔ cup superfine sugar
- 3 large egg yolks
- 1 tablespoon cornstarch
- 2½ cups milk
- 2 tablespoons finely ground espresso coffee
- 2 os semisweet chocolate, broken into pieces, plus extra shavings to decorate

Shortbread

- 1⅓ cups plus 1 tablespoon all-purpose flour
- 2 teaspoons unsweetened cocoa
- ½ cup plus 1 tablespoon (1 stick plus 1 tablespoon) unsalted butter, chilled and diced
- 2 tablespoons superfine sugar

1. Preheat the oven for 350°F. Make the shortbread. Sift the flour and cocoa into a bowl or food processor. Add the butter and cut in with a pastry blender or the fingertips or pulse with the food processor until the mixture resembles fine bread crumbs. Mix in the sugar and bring the mixture together with your hands to form a dough. Press evenly over the bottom and sides of a deep 8-inch fluted tart pan. Bake for 20 minutes, then let cool.

2. Make the filling. In a small bowl, soak the gelatin in the water. In a large bowl, whip together the sugar, egg yolks, cornstarch, and 2 tablespoons of the milk. In a saucepan, bring the remaining milk and coffee to a boil. Beat it into the egg mixture.

3. Return the mixture to the pan and heat gently, stirring continuously, until thickened. Remove from the heat and beat in the gelatin mixture until dissolved. Add the chocolate and stir until it has melted. Let cool slightly, then pour the mixture into the pie shell. Chill for several hours. Transfer the pie to a plate and scatter generously with chocolate shavings.

DEEP DISH PUFF APPLE PIE

SERVES 6

- 2 lb or about 5 baking apples, quartered, cored, peeled, and thickly sliced
- ½ cup superfine sugar, plus extra for sprinkling
- Grated zest of 1 small orange
- ½ teaspoon apple pie spice or ground cinnamon
- 3 whole cloves
- 14 oz puff pastry (see page 17 for homemade), thawed if frozen but chilled
- All-purpose flour, for dusting
- Beaten egg, to glaze

1. Fill a 5-cup pie dish with the apples. In a bowl, mix the sugar with the orange zest and spices, then sprinkle over the apples.

2. Preheat the oven to 400°F. Roll out the pastry on a lightly floured work surface until it is slightly larger than the dish and use to cover the pie (see page 9). "Scallop" the pastry edges (see page 17), then crimp (see page 10). Reroll the trimmings and use a small cookie cutter to cut out heart shapes or circles. Brush the pastry with beaten egg, add the pastry shapes, and then brush these with beaten egg. Sprinkle lightly with sugar.

3. Bake in the oven for 20-25 minutes, until the pastry is well risen and golden. Serve warm with spoonfuls of crème fraîche or extra-thick cream.

TIP

- For spiced plum & pear pie, substitute 1 lb pears, peeled, cored, and sliced, and 1 lb plums, pitted and sliced, for the apples, sprinkle with a heaping ⅓ cup superfine sugar, and add 2 halved star anise, 3 cloves, and ¼ teaspoon ground cinnamon, omitting the orange zest. Cover with the pastry and continue as above.

RHUBARB & GINGER PIE

Use young, brightly colored stalks of rhubarb, but don't forget to add sugar. No matter how appealing the color and tender the flesh, rhubarb is always sour.

SERVES 6

- 1½ lb rhubarb, sliced
- ¼ cup superfine sugar
- 3 tablespoons orange juice
- 2 teaspoons ground ginger
- 3½ tablespoons heavy cream

Pastry
- 1½ cups all-purpose flour, plus extra for dusting
- 6 tablespoons (¾ stick) butter, chilled and diced
- 2 tablespoons superfine sugar
- 1 teaspoon grated orange zest
- 1 small egg, lightly beaten
- 1–2 tablespoons ice water

1. Make the pastry. Sift the flour into a bowl or food processor. Add the butter and cut in with a pastry blender or the fingertips or pulse with the food processor until the mixture resembles fine bread crumbs. Mix in the sugar and orange zest, then add the egg and enough ice water to mix or pulse to a firm dough. Knead the dough briefly on a lightly floured work surface, then wrap in foil and chill for 30 minutes.

2. Preheat the oven to 375°F. Roll out the dough on a lightly floured work surface and use to line a 9-inch pie dish. Line the pie shell with wax paper and half-fill with dry beans or rice or pie weights. Blind bake in the oven for 20 minutes (see page 9). Lift out the paper and beans and bake for another 5 minutes. Let cool.

3. In a saucepan, combine the rhubarb, sugar, orange juice, and ginger, and simmer until the rhubarb is tender, 10–15 minutes. Spread the cream over the pie shell, then spoon over the rhubarb mixture. Serve warm.

CHOCOLATE MINCEMEAT PIES

MAKES 12

- 2¾ cups all-purpose flour, plus extra for dusting
- 3 tablespoons unsweetened cocoa
- 6 tablespoons confectioners' sugar, plus extra, sifted, for dusting
- ¾ cup plus 2 tablespoons (1½ sticks plus 2 tablespoons) butter, chilled and cubed, plus extra for greasing
- 1 extra-large egg, lightly beaten
- 1–2 tablespoons ice water
- 1½ lb sweet mincemeat
- ⅔ cup chopped pecans
- Scant ½ cup chopped semisweet chocolate
- 3 tablespoons apricot glaze or cranberry jelly

1. Sift the flour, cocoa, and confectioners' sugar into a bowl or food processor. Add the butter and cut in with a pastry blender or the fingertips or pulse with the food processor until the mixture resembles fine bread crumbs. Add the egg and enough ice water to mix or pulse to a firm dough. Knead the dough briefly on a lightly floured work surface, then wrap in foil and chill for 1 hour.

2. Grease a deep 12-cup muffin pan. Roll out the pastry on a lightly floured work surface and cut out 5-inch circles by cutting around a tartlet pan or upturned saucer. Reroll the trimmings and cut out more circles so you have 12 in total. Ease the pastry circles into the pan, letting them extend over the top edges of the cups, and chill for 15 minutes. Preheat the oven to 400°F.

3. Spoon the mincemeat into the pie shells and sprinkle over the pecans and chocolate. Press the pastry edges up and over the filling to make a rim. Brush the tops with apricot glaze or cranberry jelly and bake in the oven for 30 minutes. Let cool in the pan. Remove from the pan and dust with sifted confectioners' sugar to serve.

STICKY DATE, PEAR & TOFFEE PIE

SERVES 8

- Single quantity Rough Puff Pastry (see page 18) or 1 lb store-bought puff pastry, chilled
- All-purpose flour, for dusting
- Beaten egg, to glaze
- 2 teaspoons superfine sugar
- ¼ teaspoon ground cinnamon

Filling

- 4 ripe pears, peeled, cored, and sliced
- 1½ cups chopped pitted dates
- 4 teaspoons cornstarch
- ¾ cup toffee or caramel sauce

1. Preheat the oven to 400°F. Make the filling. In a bowl, combine the pears and dates. Sprinkle with the cornstarch and mix well.

2. Roll out a generous half of the pastry on a lightly floured work surface and use to line an 8-inch loose-bottom layer cake pan about 1¾ inches deep, letting it extend slightly over the top edges. Turn the pear mix into the pan, then spoon the sauce on top. Brush the top edges of the pastry with water. Roll out the remaining pastry with any trimmings until it is slightly larger than the pan and position on top (see page 9). Press the pastry edges together firmly to seal and trim the excess, then crimp the edges (see page 10). Brush with beaten egg, make a hole in the center of the pie, and bake in the oven for 20 minutes. Reduce the temperature to 350°F and bake for another 30 minutes, or until deep golden.

3. Mix the sugar and cinnamon together and sprinkle over the top of the pie. Let cool in the pan for 20 minutes, then transfer to a plate with a rim to catch the toffee sauce when the pie is cut. Serve with pouring cream or vanilla ice cream.

APRICOT & PISTACHIO PURSES P154

WITH A TWIST

PASTA PIE

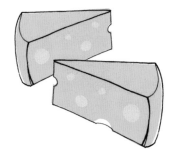

SERVES 4
- 1 tablespoon olive oil, plus extra for oiling
- 14½ oz leeks, sliced
- 2 garlic cloves, crushed
- 4 large eggs, lightly beaten
- ⅔ cup light cream
- 1¼ cups shredded Gruyère cheese
- 1 cup cooked fusilli
- Salt and black pepper

1 Preheat the oven to 350°F. Brush an ovenproof dish or medium-size cake pan with oil. In a skillet, heat the oil and sauté the leeks and garlic until soft. Mix with all the remaining ingredients, season to taste with salt and pepper, and turn into the dish or pan.

2 Bake in the oven for 25 minutes, or until the eggs have set and the pie is golden brown. Serve with a crisp green salad.

TIP

- For chicken & mozzarella macaroni pie, follow the first stage of the recipe, then add 1½ cups diced cooked chicken and 2 tablespoons finely chopped tarragon with the eggs and cream, together with 1 cup shredded mozzarella cheese and 1 cup cooked macaroni. Bake in the oven as above.

POTATO, SHALLOT & HERB PIES

MAKES 4

- 1 lb new potatoes, scrubbed and thinly sliced
- 2 tablespoons (¼ stick) butter, plus extra for greasing
- 3 shallots, thinly sliced, plus 1 large shallot, cut into 4 thick slices
- 3 garlic cloves, finely chopped
- 1 cup heavy cream
- 1 large egg yolk
- 2 tablespoons chopped chives
- 2 teaspoons chopped thyme, plus extra leaves for sprinkling
- ¼ teaspoon grated nutmeg
- 1 lb puff pastry (see page 17 for homemade), thawed if frozen but chilled
- All-purpose flour, for dusting
- 1 cup shredded Emmental cheese
- Beaten egg, to glaze
- Salt and black pepper

1. In a large saucepan, cook the potatoes in boiling water until only just tender, 3–4 minutes. Tip into a colander, drain well, and let cool. In a skillet, melt the butter and sauté the shallots and garlic until softened and just turning golden, 4–5 minutes. Let cool. In a bowl, lightly beat together the cream, egg yolk, herbs, nutmeg, and a generous amount of salt and pepper.

2. Preheat the oven to 400°F. Grease four individual 4-inch springform pans. Divide the pastry into four pieces, then roll out each piece thinly on a lightly floured work surface into a roughly shaped 8-inch circle. Use to line the pans, leaving the excess pastry hanging over the sides. Divide half the potatoes among the pans and top with the sautéed shallots, cheese, and the remaining potatoes. Cover with the cream mix, squeeze the ends of the pastry together to enclose the filling, trimming off any excess, and brush the edges with beaten egg to seal.

3. Brush the tops with beaten egg, add a slice of shallot on top, and sprinkle with thyme leaves and salt and pepper. Bake in the oven for 30–35 minutes, checking after 20 minutes and covering with foil if the pastry is overbrowning. Let stand for 5 minutes, then loosen the edges with a knife and remove the pans. Serve right away, with arugula and bacon salad, if liked.

VEGETABLE SAMOSA PIE

SERVES 6-8

- 2 tablespoons sunflower oil
- 1 onion, chopped
- 1 teaspoon cumin seed
- 1 teaspoon mustard seed
- 1 teaspoon chopped fresh ginger
- 1¼ cups grated carrots
- 2 cups grated potatoes
- Heaping 1 cup frozen green peas
- Handful of cilantro leaves, chopped
- 2 tablespoons lemon juice
- 2 teaspoons curry powder
- 1 teaspoon ground coriander
- ¼ teaspoon chili powder
- 4 tablespoons (½ stick) butter, melted, plus extra for greasing
- ½ lb phyllo dough, thawed if frozen but chilled
- Salt and black pepper

1. In a skillet, heat the oil and sauté the onion, cumin and mustard seed, and ginger until softened and lightly browned, 5 minutes. Add the carrots and potatoes and cook gently until the vegetables are tender, 6-8 minutes.

2. Add the peas, cilantro, lemon juice, curry powder, coriander, and chili powder, season with salt and pepper, and stir well. Cook for 5 minutes, stirring, then let cool slightly.

3. Preheat the oven to 400°F. Grease a large cookie sheet. Working quickly, place three sheets of phyllo down the length of the cookie sheet, overlapping each by 1 inch and brushing with melted butter—the pastry will overlap the cookie sheet. (Keep the remaining sheets of phyllo dough covered with a clean dish towel to prevent drying out.) Continue layering the phyllo until you have three layers of pastry, brushing each layer with melted butter. Put the vegetable filling on the center third of the pastry to within 1 inch of the top and bottom edges. Draw the top and bottom edges over, fold in the sides to enclose the filling, then scrunch the pastry on top.

4. Bake the pie in the oven for 25 minutes, until the pastry is golden brown and crisp. Serve with vegetables or a salad and a bowl of plain yogurt with chopped mint and cucumber.

VEGETABLE GARLIC CRUMBLE PIE

SERVES 4

- 2 tablespoons oil
- 1 garlic clove, chopped
- 1 onion, chopped
- 2 carrots, chopped
- ½ lb broccoli florets
- 14½-oz can diced tomatoes
- 1 tablespoon tomato paste
- ½ teaspoon dried oregano
- 1 teaspoon paprika
- Pinch of sugar

- 3 tablespoons water
- 15-oz can chickpeas (garbanzo beans), drained
- Salt and black pepper

Crumble

- 3 tablespoons olive oil
- 2 garlic cloves, chopped
- 1½ cups fresh brown bread crumbs
- 2 tablespoons chopped parsley

1. Preheat the oven to 400°F. In a skillet, heat the oil and sauté the garlic and onion until softened and lightly colored, about 5 minutes. Stir in the carrots and broccoli and mix well. Add the tomatoes, tomato paste, oregano, paprika, and sugar, with salt and pepper to taste. Add the water and bring to a boil. Cover and cook gently until the vegetables are just tender, 10–12 minutes. Stir in the chickpeas (garbanzo beans) and heat through.

2. Make the crumble. In a saucepan, heat the oil and gently sauté the garlic until softened, about 2 minutes. Stir in the bread crumbs and parsley with salt and pepper to taste.

3. Turn the vegetable mix into a 3¾-cup ovenproof dish and sprinkle the crumble over the top. Bake in the oven for 25 minutes, until the topping is crisp and golden brown. Serve hot with warm bread.

TARTE AU FROMAGE

This hot soufflé cheesecake is a variation of a classic French supper dish. The sauce can be prepared in advance—cover and chill until required. Serve the pie with a crisp green salad.

SERVES 4

- ½ lb store-bought pie crust (or use homemade Short-Crust Pastry—see page 14), chilled
- 4 tablespoons (½ stick) butter
- ⅓ cup plus 1 tablespoon all-purpose flour, plus extra for dusting
- 1¼ cups milk, warmed
- 2¼ cups shredded cheddar cheese

- 6 large eggs, separated
- 2 tablespoons snipped chives, plus extra to garnish
- 1 tablespoon chopped parsley, plus extra to garnish
- ½ teaspoon Tabasco sauce or to taste
- Salt and black pepper

1. Roll out the pie crust on a lightly floured work surface and use to line a deep 8-inch loose-bottom cake pan. Chill the pie shell for 30 minutes. Preheat the oven to 375°F. Line the pie shell with wax paper and half-fill with dry beans or rice or pie weights. Blind bake in the oven for 15 minutes (see page 9). Lift out the paper and beans and bake for another 5 minutes. Increase the oven temperature to 400°F.

2. In a saucepan, melt the butter and add the flour. Cook gently, stirring, for 1 minute, then remove from the heat and gradually blend in the milk. Return to the heat and cook, stirring continuously, until bubbling and thickened. Remove from the heat and let cool slightly. Beat in the cheddar and egg yolks, one at a time. Return to low heat and stir until the cheese has melted. Season to taste with salt and pepper and stir in the herbs and Tabasco.

3. In a clean, dry, grease-free bowl, whip the egg whites until they form stiff peaks, then gently fold into the cheese mixture with a large metal spoon. Immediately pour into the pie shell. Bake in the oven for 30 minutes, until well risen and golden. Carefully remove the pie from the pan, scatter with extra chopped herbs, and serve right away.

PIZZA PUFF PIES

MAKES 6

- 3 tablespoons vegetable oil plus extra (optional) for drizzling
- 1 onion, chopped
- 1 garlic clove, finely chopped
- 14½-oz can diced tomatoes
- 1 teaspoon sugar
- 1 lb puff pastry (see page 17 for homemade), thawed if frozen but chilled

- All-purpose flour, for dusting
- Small bunch of basil
- 4-oz package mozzarella cheese, drained
- 6 pitted black olives (optional)
- Salt and black pepper

1. In a saucepan, heat 2 tablespoons of the oil and sauté the onion until softened, 5 minutes. Add the garlic, tomatoes, sugar, and salt and pepper to taste. Cover and simmer gently, stirring occasionally, until the sauce has thickened, about 15 minutes. Let cool slightly.

2. Preheat the oven to 400°F. Brush six individual 4-inch tart pans 1 inch deep with oil. Divide the pastry into six pieces, then roll out each piece on a lightly floured work surface and cut out a 6-inch circle by cutting around an upturned saucer. Press each pastry circle into the bottom of a tart pan and press the pastry at intervals to the sides of the pan to give a wavy edge.

3. Reserve half the smaller basil leaves for garnish, then tear the larger leaves into pieces and stir into the sauce. Divide the sauce among the pie shells and spread into an even layer. Cut the mozzarella into six slices and add a slice to each pie. Sprinkle the mozzarella with salt and pepper, and add an olive to each, if liked. Bake in the oven for 20 minutes, until the pastry is crisp and golden. Let cool in the pans for 5 minutes, then turn out. Drizzle lightly with olive oil, if liked, sprinkle with the reserved basil leaves, and serve warm with salad.

TIP

- For mushroom & anchovy puff pies, add 1¾ cups sliced button mushrooms to the tomato sauce for the last 5 minutes of cooking. Spoon the sauce into the pies and top with the mozzarella, omitting the olives. Halve 6 canned anchovy fillets, arrange two halves as a cross on top of each pie, then bake and garnish as above.

RATATOUILLE PIE

- -

SERVES 4-6

- 1 large eggplant, cubed
- 2 tablespoons olive oil
- 1 large onion, thinly sliced
- 2 garlic cloves, chopped
- 2 red bell peppers, seeded and chopped
- 1 yellow bell pepper, seeded and chopped
- 14½-oz can diced tomatoes
- 1 tablespoon tomato paste
- 1 tablespoon torn basil leaves
- 3 zucchini, sliced
  Salt and black pepper

Pastry
- 1⅓ cups plus 1 tablespoon all-purpose flour, plus extra for dusting
- ⅓ cup (½ stick plus 1⅓ tablespoons) butter, chilled and diced
- ¼ cup grated Parmesan cheese
- Pinch of chili powder
- 1 large egg yolk
- 1–2 tablespoons ice water
- Beaten egg or milk, to glaze

1. Place the eggplant in a colander, sprinkle with salt, and let stand for 30 minutes. Rinse under cold running water, drain, and dry on paper towels. In a large saucepan, heat the oil and sauté the onion until softened, about 10 minutes. Stir in the garlic and bell peppers and sauté for 5 minutes. Stir in the eggplant, tomatoes, and tomato paste with salt and pepper to taste. Bring to a boil, then reduce the heat, cover, and simmer for 20 minutes. Add the basil and zucchini and cook for another 5 minutes. Let cool, then turn into a 5-cup pie dish.

2. Preheat the oven to 400°F. Make the pastry. Sift the flour into a bowl or food processor. Add the butter and cut in with a pastry blender or the fingertips or pulse with the food processor until the mixture resembles fine bread crumbs. Mix in the Parmesan and chili powder, then add the egg yolk and enough ice water to mix or pulse to a firm dough. Knead the dough briefly on a lightly floured work surface, then roll out thinly and cut into 1-inch wide strips with a knife or pastry wheel.

3. Brush the rim of the pie dish with water, place a pastry strip all round, and moisten with water. Arrange the pastry strips decoratively over the pie. Brush with beaten egg or milk. Bake the pie in the oven for 35–40 minutes, until the pie crust is crisp and golden brown. Serve hot.

ORIENTAL MUSHROOM POCKETS

- -

MAKES 4

- 4 large portobello mushrooms, wiped
- 1 tablespoon sesame oil
- 1 tablespoon ketjap manis or soy sauce
- 1-inch piece of fresh ginger, peeled and finely chopped
- 2 garlic cloves, finely chopped
- 4 tablespoons coarsely chopped cilantro
- 1 tomato, cut into 4 thick slices

- 2 tablespoons (¼ stick) butter, cut into 4 pieces, plus extra for greasing
- Single quantity Short-Crust Pastry (see page 14), chilled
- All-purpose flour, for dusting
- Beaten egg, to glaze
- 4 teaspoons sesame seed
- Black pepper

1. Preheat the oven to 400°F. Grease a cookie sheet. Trim the top of the mushroom stems level with the caps, drizzle the gills with the sesame oil and ketjap manis or soy sauce, then sprinkle with the ginger, garlic, and cilantro. Top each with a slice of tomato, a piece of butter, and pepper.

2. Divide the pastry into four pieces, roll out one piece thinly on a lightly floured work surface into a roughly shaped 7–8 inch circle, or large enough to enclose a mushroom (this will depend on how big they are, so make a bit larger if necessary). Place a mushroom on top of one pastry circle, brush the edges with beaten egg, then lift the pastry up and over the top of the mushroom, pleating the pastry as you go and pinching the ends together in the center of the mushroom to completely enclose it. Place on the cookie sheet. Repeat with the remaining pastry and mushrooms.

3. Brush the pockets with beaten egg and sprinkle with the sesame seed. Bake in the oven for about 25 minutes, until the pie crust is golden brown. Serve right away with stir-fried vegetables and soy sauce.

TIP

- For French mushroom pockets, drizzle 4 large portobello mushrooms with 1 tablespoon olive oil and 2 tablespoons red wine, then top with 2 finely chopped garlic cloves, 2 tablespoons each chopped basil and chives, and 4 slices of goat cheese. Season the cheese with salt and pepper, then wrap in pastry, brush with beaten egg, and top with a slice of onion. Bake as above.

CARIBBEAN CHICKEN PATTIES

MAKES 4

- 2 tablespoons sunflower oil, plus extra for oiling
- ½ lb boneless, skinless chicken breast, diced
- ½ lb butternut squash, peeled, seeded, and finely diced
- 1 small onion, chopped
- 2 garlic cloves, finely chopped
- ½ small Scotch bonnet chile, seeded and finely chopped
- 1 red or orange bell pepper, seeded and diced
- 1 teaspoon mild curry powder or paste

- 2 tablespoons chopped cilantro
- Black pepper

Pastry
- 2 cups all-purpose flour, plus extra for dusting
- 1½ teaspoons ground turmeric
- ½ cup plus 1 tablespoon (1 stick plus 1 tablespoon) vegetable shortening, chilled and diced
- 2½–3 tablespoons ice water
- Beaten egg, to glaze
- Salt

1. For the pastry, sift the flour, turmeric, and a pinch of salt into a bowl. Add the shortening and cut in with a pastry blender or fingertips or pulse with the food processor until the mixture resembles fine bread crumbs. Add enough ice water to mix or pulse to a soft but not sticky dough. Knead on a lightly floured work surface, wrap in foil and chill, and make the filling.

2. In a skillet, heat the oil and sauté the chicken and squash until the chicken is just beginning to brown, 5 minutes. Add the onion, garlic, chile, and bell pepper and sauté until the vegetables are softened and the chicken cooked through, about 5 minutes. Stir in the curry powder, cilantro, and a bit of pepper and cook briefly, then let cool.

3. Preheat the oven to 375°F. Brush a cookie sheet with oil. Divide the pastry into four pieces, roll out each piece on a lightly floured work surface and cut a 7-inch circle around an upturned plate. Divide the filling among the pastry circles and brush the edges with beaten egg. Fold in half and press the edges together to seal, then press the edges with a fork. Transfer to the cookie sheet, brush the patties with beaten egg, and bake in the oven for 20–25 minutes, until golden. Serve hot or cold with chutney.

INDIAN SPICED BEEF TURNOVERS

MAKES 6

- 2 tablespoons vegetable oil, plus extra for oiling
- 1 onion, chopped
- 2 carrots, diced
- 1 lb ground beef
- 2 teaspoons lightly crushed cumin seed
- 2 teaspoons lightly crushed fennel seed
- 2 garlic cloves, crushed
- 1 medium-strength red chile, seeded and finely chopped
- ½ teaspoon ground turmeric
- ½ teaspoon ground cinnamon
- 1 oz creamed coconut
- 4 tablespoons water
- 4 tablespoons finely chopped cilantro
- 7 oz tomatoes, skinned and roughly chopped
- 1 tablespoon garam masala
- Single quantity Potato Pastry (see page 20), chilled
- All-purpose flour, for dusting
- Beaten egg, to glaze
- Salt (optional)

1. In a skillet, heat the oil and gently sauté the onion and carrots until beginning to color, 10 minutes. Add the beef and cook, stirring and breaking up with a wooden spoon, until evenly browned, 6–8 minutes. Add the cumin, fennel, garlic, chile, turmeric, cinnamon, creamed coconut, and water. Cook gently, stirring, until the coconut has melted into the mixture, another 5 minutes. Remove from the heat and stir in the cilantro, tomatoes, and garam masala. Season to taste with salt, if necessary, and let cool.

2. Preheat the oven to 400°F. Brush a large cookie sheet with oil. Divide the pastry into six pieces and roll out each piece on a lightly floured work surface into a roughly shaped 8-inch circle. Brush the edges of the pastry circles with beaten egg and spoon the filling down the center of each pastry circle. Bring the edges of the pastry up over the filling and press together firmly, then crimp (see page 10). Transfer to the cookie sheet.

3. Brush the turnovers with beaten egg and bake in the oven for 25–30 minutes, until deep golden.

CRISPY DUCK PUFFS

These individual pies have a distinctly Oriental flavor partly because of the hoisin sauce, which is a common ingredient in many Southeast Asian dishes. Serve hot or cold.

MAKES 6

- Sunflower oil, for oiling
- ¾ lb puff pastry (see page 17 for homemade), thawed if frozen but chilled
- All-purpose flour, for dusting
- Beaten egg or milk, to glaze
- 2 duck legs

- 6 tablespoons crème fraîche or thick sour cream
- 8 tablespoons hoisin sauce
- 6 scallions, thinly sliced
- ½ cucumber, cut into matchsticks
- ¼ cup cilantro leaves

1. Brush a cookie sheet with oil. Divide the pastry into six pieces, then roll out each piece on a lightly floured work surface and trim into a 4-inch square. Make two "L"-shape cuts in the pastry 1 inch in from the edge, leaving the two opposite corners uncut. Brush the edges of the pastry squares with water. Lift up one cut corner of each pastry square and draw it across the pastry to the opposite cut side. Repeat with the other cut side to form a pie shell. Brush the edges of the pastry with egg or milk, prick the bottom, and place on the cookie sheet. Chill while you prepare the duck.

2. Preheat the oven to 400°F. Prick the duck legs with a fork and place on a rack set over a roasting pan to catch the fat. Roast for 30 minutes. Let cool, then shred the meat and skin from the duck legs.

3. In a bowl, mix the duck meat with the crème fraîche or sour cream and hoisin sauce, then divide among the pie shells. Bake in the oven for 25 minutes, until the pastry has risen and is golden on top. Combine the scallions, cucumber, and cilantro, then arrange the mixture on top of the pies just before serving, hot or cold.

MUSTARD POTATO & PASTRAMI PIES

MAKES 4

- 1 lb new potatoes, scrubbed and thinly sliced
- 2 tablespoons (¼ stick) butter, plus extra for greasing
- 3 shallots, thinly sliced, plus 1 large shallot, cut into 4 thick slices
- 3 garlic cloves, finely chopped
- 1 cup heavy cream
- 1 large egg yolk
- 2 teaspoons whole grain mustard
- 1 lb puff pastry (see page 17 for homemade), thawed if frozen but chilled
- All-purpose flour, for dusting
- 3½ oz sliced pastrami
- Beaten egg, to glaze
- Salt and black pepper

1. In a saucepan, cook the potatoes in boiling water until only just tender, 3–4 minutes. Tip into a colander and drain well. In a skillet, melt the butter and sauté the shallots and garlic until softened and just turning golden, 4–5 minutes. In a bowl, beat together the cream, egg yolk, mustard, and a generous amount of salt and pepper.

2. Preheat the oven to 400°F. Grease four individual 4-inch springform pans. Divide the pastry into four pieces, then roll out each piece thinly on a lightly floured work surface into a roughly shaped 8-inch circle and use to line the pans, leaving the excess pastry hanging over the sides. Divide half the potatoes among the pie shells and top with the sautéed shallots and garlic, the pastrami, and the remaining potatoes. Cover with the mustard cream mix, squeeze the ends of the pastry together to enclose the filling, trimming off any excess, and brush the edges with beaten egg to seal.

3. Brush the tops of the pies with beaten egg, add a slice of shallot on top, and sprinkle with salt and pepper. Bake in the oven for 30–35 minutes, until the pie crust is golden brown, covering the tops with foil if the pastry is browning too quickly. Let cool in the pans for 5 minutes, then loosen the edges with a knife, remove the pans, and serve hot.

SWEET POTATO & CHORIZO PIE

Chorizo is a Spanish pork sausage, traditionally flavored with red bell peppers. It's a wonderful complement to the sweet potato.

SERVES 4

- 1½ lb sweet potato, peeled and cut into 1-inch cubes
- 1 large red bell pepper, seeded and cut into 1-inch cubes
- 3 garlic cloves, left in their skins
- 2 tablespoons olive oil, plus extra for oiling
- 5 oz chorizo, cut into ½-inch cubes
- ½ cup ricotta cheese
- 1 cup shredded cheddar cheese
- 2 tablespoons crème fraîche or thick sour cream
- 2 large egg yolks
- ¾ lb store-bought pie crust (or use homemade Short-Crust Pastry—see page 14), chilled
- All-purpose flour, for dusting
- Beaten egg, to glaze
- 3 rosemary sprigs
- Salt and black pepper

1. Preheat the oven to 400°F. In a roasting dish, combine the sweet potato, bell pepper, and garlic cloves. Drizzle with olive oil, season with salt and pepper, and roast in the oven for 15 minutes. Add the chorizo and roast for another 5–10 minutes, until the vegetables are slightly golden. Let cool.

2. Push the garlic pulp out of the skins and place in a bowl with the ricotta, cheddar, crème fraîche or sour cream, and egg yolks. Beat together until smooth.

3. Brush a cookie sheet with oil. Roll out the pie crust on a lightly floured work surface into a roughly shaped 12-inch circle and transfer to the cookie sheet. Brush the pastry with beaten egg. Spoon the ricotta mixture into the center, leaving a 3-inch border around the sides. Place the roasted vegetables and chorizo on top of the ricotta mixture.

4. Fold in the pastry border so it partly overlaps the filling. Brush the sides with more beaten egg. Scatter with the rosemary sprigs and season to taste with salt and pepper. Bake in the oven for 30–35 minutes, until the pie crust is golden.

COCKLE, LEEK & BACON PIES

MAKES 6

- 2½ cups milk
- 7 oz leeks, thinly sliced, white and green parts kept separate
- 2 bay leaves
- ½-lb ready-to-cook center-cut ham steak
- 4 tablespoons (½ stick) butter
- ⅓ cup plus 1 tablespoon all-purpose flour
- 7 oz shelled cockles or small clams, thawed if frozen
- Salt and black pepper

Pastry
- 3 cups all-purpose flour, plus extra for dusting
- ¾ cup (1½ sticks) mixed butter and vegetable shortening, chilled and diced, plus extra for greasing
- 4–4½ tablespoons ice water
- Beaten egg, to glaze

1. In a saucepan, combine the milk, white leek parts, bay leaves, and salt and pepper, then bring to a boil. Remove from the heat and let stand for 10 minutes, then strain, reserving the leeks and milk separately. Cook the ham steak under a hot broiler in a pan lined with foil until cooked through, turning once, 7–8 minutes. Trim off the fat, then dice the meat.

2. In a saucepan, melt the butter and add the flour. Cook gently, stirring, for 1 minute, then remove from the heat and gradually blend in the strained milk. Return to the heat and cook, stirring continuously, until bubbling and thickened. Add the reserved white leek parts with the green leek parts and cook gently, stirring, until the leeks are just cooked, 2–3 minutes. Let cool.

3. Make the pastry. Sift the flour into a bowl or food processor and season with salt and pepper. Add the butter and shortening and cut in with a pastry blender or the fingertips or pulse with the food processor until the mixture resembles fine bread crumbs. Add enough ice water to mix or pulse to a firm dough. Wrap in foil and chill for 15 minutes.

4. Preheat the oven to 375°F. Grease six individual 4-inch tart pans 1 inch deep. Reserve one-third of the pastry. Divide the remaining pastry into six pieces, then roll out each piece on a lightly floured work surface and cut out six 6-inch circles by cutting around a tartlet pan or upturned saucer.

Use to line the pans, letting the pastry extend slightly over the top edges. Stir the cockles and ham into the sauce, then spoon into the pie shells.

5. Roll out the reserved pastry with any trimmings and cut out six 5-inch circles in the same way. Brush the top edges of the pie shells with beaten egg, position the pastry circles on top, and press the edges together firmly to seal, then crimp (see page 10). Brush the tops with beaten egg and prick to let the steam escape. Decorate with pastry trimmings (see page 11) and sprinkle with salt and pepper. Place on a cookie sheet and bake for 30–35 minutes, until golden brown.

SALMON & ASPARAGUS EN CROÛTE

SERVES 4

- 2 tablespoons (¼ stick) butter
- 6 oz asparagus spears, trimmed
- About 1¼ lb salmon fillet, about 7–8 inches long, skinned
- Juice of ½ lemon
- 1 lb puff pastry (see page 17 for homemade), thawed if frozen but chilled
- All-purpose flour, for dusting
- Scant ½ cup medium-fat soft cheese
- Grated zest of 1 lemon

- 1 tablespoon chopped tarragon
- 2 tablespoons chopped parsley
- 1½ teaspoons green peppercorns, drained and chopped (optional)
- ¼ cup semi-dried tomatoes in oil, drained and coarsely chopped
- Beaten egg, to glaze
- Salt flakes, for sprinkling (optional)
- Salt and black pepper
- Lemon wedges, to serve

1. In a skillet, melt the butter and sauté the asparagus until just softened, 2–3 minutes, then season to taste with salt and pepper. Drizzle the salmon with lemon juice and season.

2. Preheat the oven to 400°F. Roll the pastry out thinly on a lightly floured surface and trim to a 14-inch square, then trim a 1½-inch strip from one of the sides. Put the salmon on top so the long side of the salmon is parallel with the narrower side of the pastry rectangle. Dot the cheese on top of the salmon, then sprinkle with the lemon zest, herbs, peppercorns, if using, and tomatoes. Arrange the asparagus on top, alternating their direction. Brush the pastry around the salmon with beaten egg, then fold the narrower sides up and over the salmon, pressing to seal. Trim the excess from the top ends of the pastry, then fold and press to wrap the salmon like a parcel.

3. Brush the parcel with beaten egg and transfer to a cookie sheet. Decorate with pastry trimmings (see page 11) and sprinkle with salt flakes, if liked. Bake in the oven for 35–40 minutes, covering with foil if the pastry seems to be browning too quickly. To test if the salmon is cooked, insert a knife into the center, wait 3 seconds, then remove; if the knife feels hot, it is cooked. Cut into thick slices and serve with lemon wedges.

POTATO, HAM & ARTICHOKE PIE

This freeform pie has a moist, sconelike dough, which is perfect for all sorts of savory toppings.

SERVES 4

- ⅓ cup (½ stick plus 1⅓ tablespoons) butter, plus extra for greasing
- 1 onion, thinly sliced
- 1¼ cups all-purpose flour
- ⅔ cup mashed potatoes
- 1 tablespoon olive oil
- 2 shallots, sliced
- 1¾ cups sliced white mushrooms
- 4 oz cooked ham, cut into strips
- 6 oz drained canned artichoke hearts, sliced
- Salt and black pepper
- Thyme sprigs, to garnish

1. In a saucepan, melt 2 tablespoons (¼ stick) of the butter and sauté the onion until softened and lightly browned. Let cool slightly.

2. Preheat the oven to 400°F. Grease a cookie sheet. Sift the flour into a bowl or food processor. Dice the remaining butter and cut it into the flour with a pastry blender or the fingertips, or pulse with the food processor until the mixture resembles fine bread crumbs. Add the sautéed onion with the pan juices and the mashed potatoes and season to taste with salt and pepper. Mix to a soft dough. Press out the dough on the cookie sheet into a 9-inch circle. Pinch the edges of the dough to make a rim.

3. In a skillet, heat the oil and sauté the shallots until lightly browned. Add the mushrooms and cook briefly until softened. Scatter the ham and artichokes over the dough, then top with the shallot and mushroom mixture. Season again, if liked, and bake in the oven for 25–30 minutes, until the pastry is golden brown. Serve hot, garnished with thyme sprigs.

MEXICAN PIE

SERVES 4

- 2 tablespoons olive oil
- 1 onion, finely chopped
- 2 garlic cloves, crushed
- 2 carrots, diced
- ½ lb ground beef
- 1 red chile, finely chopped
- 14½-oz can diced tomatoes

- 15-oz can kidney beans, drained and rinsed
- 2 oz tortilla chips
- Heaping 1 cup shredded cheddar cheese
- Salt and black pepper
- Chopped parsley or cilantro, to garnish

1. Preheat the oven to 400°F. In a saucepan, heat the oil and sauté the onion, garlic, and carrots until softened. Add the beef and chile and cook, stirring and breaking up with a wooden spoon, until the meat is evenly browned, 5 minutes. Add the tomatoes and kidney beans, mix well, and season to taste with salt and pepper.

2. Transfer to an ovenproof dish, cover with the tortilla chips, and sprinkle with the cheddar. Bake in the oven for about 20 minutes, until golden brown. Garnish with chopped parsley or cilantro before serving.

TIP

- For tortilla-wrapped chili with guacamole, follow the first stage above, but then cover and simmer for 20 minutes. Meanwhile, halve 2 large, ripe avocados lengthwise and discard the pits. Scoop the flesh into a bowl, add 3 tablespoons lime juice, and coarsely mash. Add 4 oz tomatoes, skinned, seeded, and chopped, 2 crushed garlic cloves, ½ cup chopped scallions, 1 tablespoon finely chopped green chiles, and 2 tablespoons chopped cilantro leaves, mix well, and season to taste with salt and pepper. Divide the chili among 4 warmed flour tortillas and wrap up. Serve with the guacamole and sour cream if liked.

SPICED PORK & DUCK PIE

SERVES 6

- 6 whole star anise
- ½ teaspoon salt
- 2 bay leaves, torn into pieces
- 1 teaspoon ground black pepper
- 1¾ lb pork tenderloin
- 1½ lb duck pieces, such as mixed leg, wing, and breast
- 3 tablespoons all-purpose flour, plus extra for dusting
- 4 tablespoons vegetable oil

- 2 onions, chopped
- 2 celery stalks, diced
- 3 garlic cloves, crushed
- 2 cups chicken stock
- 5 oz sliced shiitake or crimini mushrooms, sliced
- 1 lb puff pastry (see page 17 for homemade), thawed if frozen but chilled
- Beaten egg, to glaze

1. Break the star anise into pieces and place in a coffee or spice grinder, or a small food processor, with the salt, bay leaves, and pepper. Grind to a powder. Cut the pork into chunks, discarding any areas of excess fat. Quarter the duck breasts and cut the leg joints. Toss the meat in the flour.

2. Preheat the oven to 325°F. In a skillet, heat 2 tablespoons of the oil and brown the meat on all sides in batches, lifting the batches out with a slotted spoon into a casserole dish. Heat another 1 tablespoon of oil in the pan and sauté the onions and celery until softened, about 5 minutes, adding the garlic toward the end of cooking. Tip in any flour left on the plate. Blend in the stock and bring to a boil. Stir in the spice powder and pour over the meat in the casserole, cover, and cook in the oven for 1¼ hours, until the meat is very tender.

3. Meanwhile, in a skillet, heat the remaining oil and sauté the mushrooms until pale golden, 5 minutes. Add to the casserole dish and season to taste if necessary. Let cool, then turn into a pie dish. Roll out the pastry on a lightly floured work surface and cut out 2-inch wide strips. Brush the rim of the pie dish with water. Lay the strips diagonally over the dish, overlapping each by about ¾ inch and brushing the overlap with beaten egg. Trim the excess pastry, then brush with beaten egg, make a slit in the center of the pie, and bake in the oven for about 40 minutes, until the crust is golden.

ASIAN FISH PIE

SERVES 5-6

- 1 tablespoon cornstarch
- 2 tablespoons cold water
- 2 tablespoons vegetable oil
- 2 garlic cloves, thinly sliced
- 1 oz fresh ginger, peeled and grated
- 1 bunch scallions, finely chopped
- 13½-oz can coconut milk
- ⅔ cup fish stock
- 1¾ lb skinless white fish or salmon fillets, cut into pieces
- 7 oz squid rings
- 1 tablespoon light soy sauce
- ⅓ cup chopped cilantro
- 2 lb mealy potatoes, peeled and cut into chunks
- 1 hot red chile, finely chopped
- Salt

1. In a small bowl, blend the cornstarch with the water to a paste. In a saucepan, heat the oil and gently sauté the garlic and ginger for 1 minute. Stir in the scallions and sauté for another minute. Add ¾ cup of the coconut milk, the stock, and the cornstarch paste. Bring to a boil, stirring, and cook until slightly thickened. Remove from the heat, stir in the fish, squid, soy sauce, and cilantro, and turn into a shallow ovenproof dish.

2. Preheat the oven to 375°F. In a saucepan, cook the potatoes in lightly salted water until tender, about 15 minutes. Drain and return to the pan. Add the chile and remaining coconut milk and mash until completely smooth.

3. Spoon the mash over the filling, spreading it in an even layer. Fluff up with a fork. Bake in the oven for about 40 minutes, until pale golden.

APPLE & RAISIN DUMPLINGS

MAKES 4

- 4 baking apples
- 1 tablespoon lemon juice
- 2 tablespoons raw brown sugar
- 2 tablespoons (¼ stick) butter, diced
- ⅓ cup raisins
- ½ teaspoon apple pie spice

Pastry
- 2 cups all-purpose flour, plus extra for dusting

- ½ cup plus 1 tablespoon (1 stick plus 1 tablespoon) butter, chilled and diced
- 2 tablespoons superfine sugar, plus extra for sprinkling
- 1 large egg yolk
- 3–4 tablespoons ice water
- 1 large egg white, lightly beaten

1. Peel and core the apples, then brush them with lemon juice to prevent them discoloring. In a bowl, combine the brown sugar, butter, raisins, and spice and set aside.

2. Preheat the oven to 400°F. Make the pastry. Sift the flour into a bowl or food processor. Add the butter and cut in with a pastry blender or the fingertips or pulse with the food processor until the mixture resembles fine bread crumbs. Mix in the superfine sugar, then add the egg yolk and enough ice water to mix or pulse to a firm dough.

3. Knead the dough briefly on a lightly floured work surface. Divide into four pieces and roll out each piece into a 6-inch square. Place a peeled and cored apple in the center of each of the squares and fill with the raisin mixture. Brush the edges of the pastry with water, then draw up over the apple to enclose it completely.

4. Place the dumplings on a cookie sheet and brush with the egg white. Sprinkle thickly with superfine sugar and bake in the oven for 40–45 minutes, until the pastry is golden brown. Serve hot with cream or custard.

ALASKA CRUMBLE PIE

SERVES 4-6

- 3 egg whites
- ¾ cup plus 2 tablespoons superfine sugar
- 1 cup raspberries
- Heaping 1 cup red currants or scant 1 cup blackberries
- 18 oz vanilla ice cream

Crumb crust

- 6 oz oat cookies
- ⅓ cup (½ stick plus 1⅓ tablespoons) butter

1. Make the crust. In a food processor, process the cookies to crumbs. Alternatively, place them between two sheets of wax paper and crush with a rolling pin. In a saucepan, melt the butter, then mix with the cookie crumbs. Press evenly over the bottom and sides of a 9-inch pie plate or tart pan and chill until ready to serve.

2. Preheat the oven to 400°F. In a clean, dry, grease-free bowl, whip the egg whites until stiff and dry. Beat in 1 tablespoon of the sugar, then fold in the remainder with a large metal spoon.

3. Fill the pie shell with the fruit and add the ice cream in scoops. Spread the meringue over the top, covering the filling completely. Bake in the oven for 5–8 minutes, until the meringue is golden. Serve right away.

CHERRY ALMOND TURNOVERS

MAKES 8
- ¾ lb cherries, halved and pitted
- ¼ cup superfine sugar
- ½ cup ground almonds
- Few drops of almond extract
- 1 large egg white, lightly beaten

Pastry
- 2 cups all-purpose flour, plus extra for dusting
- ½ cup plus 1 tablespoon (1 stick plus 1 tablespoon) butter, chilled and diced
- 2 tablespoons superfine sugar
- 1 large egg yolk
- 3–4 tablespoons ice water
- Milk, to glaze

1. Preheat the oven to 400°F. Make the pastry. Sift the flour into a bowl or food processor. Add the butter and cut in with a pastry blender or the fingertips or pulse with the food processor until the mixture resembles fine bread crumbs. Mix in the sugar, then add the egg yolk and enough ice water to mix or pulse to a firm dough. Knead the dough briefly on a lightly floured work surface.

2. In a bowl, combine the cherries, sugar, ground almonds, almond extract, and egg white. Divide the dough into eight pieces, then roll out each piece on a lightly floured work surface into a roughly shaped 5-inch circle. Divide the filling among the pastry circles and brush the edges of the pastry lightly with water. Draw up the pastry over the filling and press the edges together firmly to seal, then crimp (see page 10).

3. Place the turnovers on a cookie sheet and brush with milk. Bake in the oven for 25 minutes, until golden brown. Serve warm or cold.

PEACH MELBA PIE

SERVES 6

- Butter, for greasing
- Single quantity Pâte Sucrée (see page 16), chilled
- All-purpose flour, for dusting
- Heaping ⅓ cup superfine sugar, plus extra for sprinkling
- 1 teaspoon cornstarch
- Grated zest of 1 lemon
- 1½ lb peaches, halved, pitted, and sliced
- 1¼ cups raspberries
- Milk, to glaze

1. Preheat the oven to 375°F. Grease an 8-inch round pie dish 2 inches deep. Reserve one-third of the pastry for the lattice. Roll out the remainder on a lightly floured work surface and use to line the dish.

2. In a bowl, combine the sugar, cornstarch, and lemon zest, then add the fruits and toss together gently. Pile into the pie shell. Roll out the reserved pastry with any trimmings thinly on a lightly floured work surface, cut into strips, and use to create a lattice top for the pie (see page 10). Brush the pastry with milk and bake in the oven for 30–35 minutes, until the pastry is golden brown.

3. Let the pie cool for 15 minutes, then cut into wedges and serve drizzled with melba sauce (see Tip).

TIP

- For melba sauce, to serve as an accompaniment, in a saucepan, combine 1⅔ cups raspberries with the juice of 1½ lemon and 2 tablespoons confectioners' sugar. Cook gently until the raspberries are just tender, 2–3 minutes. Let cool, then purée in a food processor or blender and push through a strainer to remove the seeds. Serve warm or cold with wedges of pie.

PEACH STRUDEL FINGERS

- -

MAKES 4

- 3 ripe peaches, pitted and thinly sliced
- 2 tablespoons superfine sugar
- 2 tablespoons ground almonds
- ½ teaspoon ground cinnamon
- 2 tablespoons golden raisins
- 6 sheets of phyllo dough, 12 inches x 7 inches each, thawed if frozen but chilled
- 3 tablespoons unsalted butter, melted
- Sifted confectioners' sugar, for dusting
- 2 tablespoons slivered almonds

1. Preheat the oven to 350°F. In a bowl, place the peaches, superfine sugar, ground almonds, cinnamon, and golden raisins and toss gently together.

2. Working quickly, lay one sheet of phyllo dough on a work surface, with one long edge toward you, and brush with a little of the melted butter. (Keep the remaining sheets of phyllo dough covered with a clean dish towel to prevent from drying out.) Spoon a quarter of the peach mixture horizontally (or follow the long edge) in a line down the center, stopping about 2 inches from either end. Fold the short sides of the pastry over the filling. Fold one long side over the filling, then roll up to enclose the filling completely. Transfer the strudel to a cookie sheet. Repeat to make three more strudels.

3. Cut the remaining phyllo sheets in half. Brush the outside edges of the strudels with a bit more butter, then roll up in the remaining phyllo sheets. Brush with the remaining butter and sprinkle with the slivered almonds. Bake in the oven for 10-13 minutes, until golden brown. Dust with sifted confectioners' sugar and serve warm with whipped cream or crème fraîche.

GATEAU PITHIVIERS
WITH PLUMS

SERVES 6

- 7 tablespoons (½ stick plus 3 tablespoons) unsalted butter, softened
- ½ cup superfine sugar
- 1 cup ground almonds
- Few drops of almond extract
- 1 large egg, lightly beaten

- 1 lb puff pastry (see page 17 for homemade), thawed if frozen but chilled
- All-purpose flour, for dusting
- ¾ lb plums, pitted and thickly sliced
- Beaten egg, to glaze
- Sifted confectioners' sugar, for dusting

1. Preheat the oven to 400°F. In a bowl, beat the butter and sugar together until pale and smooth. Add the almonds and almond extract, then the egg, and mix together until smooth.

2. Roll out half the pastry thinly on a lightly floured work surface and trim to a 10-inch circle by cutting round an upturned dinner plate. Place on a cookie sheet dampened with water, then spread the almond paste over the top, leaving a 1-inch border of pastry around the edges. Arrange the plums in a single layer on top. Brush the pastry border lightly with beaten egg.

3. Roll out the remaining pastry thinly and trim to a circle slightly larger than the first. Cut five or six swirly "S" shapes out of the center of the pastry, then position over the almond paste. Press the edges together to seal and trim the excess pastry if necessary. "Scallop" the pastry edges (see page 17), brush the top with beaten egg, and bake in the oven for 25–30 minutes, until well risen and golden. Let cool slightly, then dust the top with sifted confectioners' sugar and serve in wedges with cream.

TIP

- For brandied prune pithiviers, soak a scant 1 cup pitted prunes in 3 tablespoons brandy, then arrange over the almond paste instead of the plums. Continue as above.

MERINGUE MINCEMEAT PIES

MAKES 18

- ¾ lb sweet mincemeat
- 2 egg whites
- ⅔ cup superfine sugar

Pastry
- 1⅓ cup plus 1 tablespoon all-purpose flour, plus extra for dusting
- ⅓ cup whole-wheat flour
- ½ cup plus 1 tablespoon (1 stick plus 1 tablespoon) butter, chilled and diced
- ½ cup ground almonds
- 2 teaspoons grated lemon zest
- ¼ cup superfine sugar
- 1 large egg yolk
- 2–3 tablespoons lemon juice

1. Preheat the oven to 375°F. Make the pastry. Sift the flours into a bowl or food processor. Add the butter and cut in with a pastry blender or the fingertips or pulse with the food processor until the mixture resembles fine bread crumbs. Mix in the ground almonds, lemon zest, and sugar, then add the egg yolk and enough lemon juice to mix or pulse to a firm dough.

2. Knead the dough briefly on a lightly floured work surface. Roll out thinly and use a 3-inch cookie cutter to cut out 18 circles. Use the pastry circles to line 18 cups of one or two standard-size muffin/cupcake pans. Fill with the mincemeat.

3. In a clean, dry, grease-free bowl, whip the egg whites until stiff and dry, then fold in the sugar with a large metal spoon. Pile a bit of the meringue into each pie shell, covering the mincemeat filling completely. Bake in the oven for 25–30 minutes, until the pies are golden brown and the meringue is crisp. Serve warm or cold.

BABY BANANA & PEACH STRUDELS

MAKES 8

- 2 bananas, about 6 oz each with skin on, peeled and chopped
- 2 tablespoons lemon juice
- 2 small ripe peaches, about 3½ oz each, halved, pitted, and sliced
- ⅔ cup blueberries
- 2 tablespoons superfine sugar

- 2 tablespoons fresh white bread crumbs
- ½ teaspoon ground cinnamon
- 6 sheets of phyllo dough, 19 inches x 9 inches each, thawed if frozen but chilled
- 4 tablespoons (½ stick) butter, melted
- Sifted confectioners' sugar, for dusting

1. Preheat the oven to 375°F. Toss the bananas in the lemon juice, then place in a large bowl with the peach slices and blueberries. In a small bowl, combine the sugar, bread crumbs, and cinnamon, then toss with the fruit.

2. Working quickly, lay one sheet of phyllo dough on a work surface, with the one long edge toward you. (Keep the remaining sheets of phyllo dough covered with a clean dish towel to prevent drying out.) Cut in half to make two 9 inch x 10 inch rectangles. Put 2 heaping spoonfuls of the fruit mixture on each, then fold in the sides, brush the pastry with a bit of the melted butter, and roll up like a parcel. Repeat to make eight mini strudels using four sheets of phyllo.

3. Brush the strudels with a bit more melted butter. Cut the remaining pastry sheets into wide strips, then wrap them like bandages around the strudels, covering any tears or splits in the pastry. Place on a cookie sheet and brush with the remaining butter. Bake in the oven for 15-18 minutes, until golden brown and crisp. Let cool on the cookie sheet, then dust with sifted confectioners' sugar and serve. These are best eaten on the day they are made.

TIP

- For traditional apple strudels, replace the bananas and peaches with 1 lb cored, peeled, and sliced baking apples tossed with 2 tablespoons lemon juice and mixed with ⅓ cup golden raisins. Replace the bread crumbs with 2 tablespoons ground almonds and combine with cinnamon. Increase the sugar quantity to ¼ cup and continue as above.

MANGO PIE

- -

SERVES 6
- Butter, for greasing
- 1 lb puff pastry (see page 17 for homemade), thawed if frozen but chilled
- All-purpose flour, for dusting
- 2 ripe mangoes
- 2 tablespoons lime juice
- 2 oz creamed coconut, grated
- 2 tablespoons raw brown sugar
- Beaten egg, to glaze
- Superfine sugar, for sprinkling

1. Preheat the oven to 425°F. Grease a cookie sheet. Roll out half the pastry on a lightly floured work surface into a 12-inch circle. Make "V"-shaped cuts all round to form a star shape. Roll out the remaining pastry into another 12-inch circle and place the star-shaped pastry on top. Using a sharp knife, cut the lower piece of pastry into a star shape, using the upper piece as a template.

2. Peel, halve, and pit the mangoes. Cut them into thin slices. Place one piece of pastry on the cookie sheet and arrange the mango slices on top to within ½ inch of the edges. Sprinkle with the lime juice, coconut, and brown sugar. Brush the edges of the pastry with water and cover with the remaining piece of pastry. Press the edges together firmly to seal.

3. Brush the top of the pie with beaten egg and sprinkle with superfine sugar. Bake in the oven for 20–25 minutes, until risen and golden brown. Serve hot.

CHOCOLATE CREAM PIE

SERVES 6-8

- Butter, for greasing
- Single quantity chocolate Pâte Sucrée (see page 16) made by replacing 2 tablespoons of the flour with unsweetened cocoa, chilled
- 5 oz plain dark chocolate, broken into pieces
- 2 cups medium-fat soft cheese, softened
- ½ cup superfine sugar
- 1 tablespoon all-purpose flour, plus extra for dusting
- 1 teaspoon vanilla extract
- 3 large eggs

1. Grease a 9-inch fluted loose-bottom tart pan 1½ inches deep. Roll out the pastry thinly on a lightly floured work surface and use to line the pan. Trim the excess pastry with kitchen shears so it stands a bit above the top of the pan. Prick the bottom with a fork, then chill the pie shell for 15 minutes. Preheat the oven to 350°F.

2. Line the pie shell with wax paper and half-fill with dry beans or rice or pie weights. Blind bake in the oven for 15 minutes (see page 9). Lift out the paper and beans and bake for another 5 minutes. Remove from the oven and reduce the temperature to 300°F.

3. Meanwhile, in a large heatproof bowl set over a saucepan of gently simmering water, melt the chocolate. In a bowl, combine the cream cheese with the sugar, flour, and vanilla extract, then gradually beat in the eggs until smooth. Ladle about one-third into the chocolate bowl and mix until smooth.

4. Pour the vanilla cheese mixture into the pie shell, then pipe the chocolate mixture over the top and swirl together with the handle of a teaspoon for a marbled effect. Bake in the oven for 30–35 minutes, until set around the edges, beginning to crack, and the center still wobbles slightly. Let cool in the turned-off oven, then chill overnight. Remove the pie from the pan and serve cut into wedges.

DOUBLE CHOCOLATE ICE CREAM PIE

SERVES 8

- 18 oz good-quality chocolate ice cream
- ⅓ cup olive oil spread, plus extra for greasing
- 7 oz semisweet chocolate graham crackers, crushed into coarse crumbs
- 2 large bananas, sliced
- 1 tablespoon lemon juice
- 1 king-size caramel chocolate bar, cut into thin slices

1. Remove the ice cream from the freezer and let it soften. Grease and line the bottom of an 8-inch fluted loose-bottom tart pan with parchment paper. In a saucepan, melt the olive oil spread, then mix with the cracker crumbs. Press evenly over the bottom of the pan.

2. In a bowl, toss the bananas in the lemon juice, then scatter over the cracker crust. Spread the ice cream on top of the bananas, using a palette knife to evenly cover them. Scatter the chocolate bar slices over the top of the ice cream.

3. Freeze the pie for at least 1 hour before serving.

TIP

- For banoffee ice cream pie, use 7 oz plain graham crackers instead of the chocolate graham crackers and top with 13.4-oz can dulce de leche. Add the bananas in lemon juice and finish as above, using 18 oz good-quality caramel ice cream instead of the chocolate ice cream.

CHOCOLATE MOUSSE PIES

Make sure you buy the best-quality unsweetened chocolate for these pies, because the flavor is crucial. Look for chocolate with 70 percent cocoa solids.

MAKES 10

- Single quantity Rich Short-Crust Pastry (see page 15), chilled
- All-purpose flour, for dusting
- 6 oz unsweetened chocolate, broken into pieces, plus shavings to decorate
- 2–3 tablespoons water
- 1 tablespoon unsalted butter, diced
- 1 tablespoon brandy or Cointreau
- 3 large eggs, separated

1. Roll out the pastry on a lightly floured work surface and use to line eight individual 4-inch tartlet pans. Reroll the trimmings and line another two pans. Chill for 15 minutes. Preheat the oven to 400°F. Line the pie shells with wax paper and half-fill with dry beans or rice or pie weights. Blind bake in the oven for 15 minutes (see page 9). Lift out the paper and beans and bake for another 5 minutes. Let cool.

2. In a large heatproof bowl set over a saucepan of gently simmering water, melt the chocolate with the water, stirring occasionally. Remove the bowl from the pan and stir in the butter until melted. Add the brandy or Cointreau, then stir in the egg yolks. In a separate clean, dry, grease-free bowl, whip the egg whites until stiff and dry, then fold into the chocolate mixture with a large metal spoon.

3. Spoon the mousse mixture into the pie shells. Chill until set, 2–3 hours. Sprinkle with the chocolate shavings and serve cold.

COCONUT & PASSION FRUIT CHOUX BUNS

- -

MAKES ABOUT 12
- Butter, for greasing
- Single quantity Choux Pastry (see page 22)
- 1¼ cups heavy cream
- 2 oz creamed coconut
- 1⅔ cups confectioners' sugar, plus 4 tablespoons
- 2 small passion fruit

1. Preheat the oven to 400°F. Lightly grease a large cookie sheet and dampen with water. Place dessertspoonfuls of the choux pastry mixture on the cookie sheet, spacing them slightly apart. Bake in the oven for 20-25 minutes, until well risen and deep golden. Make a horizontal slit along one side of each bun and bake for another 3 minutes. Transfer to a wire rack to cool.

2. In a saucepan, combine half the cream with the creamed coconut and the 4 tablespoons confectioners' sugar. Heat gently until the coconut has melted. Pour into a bowl and let cool. Add the remaining cream and whip the mixture until just holding its shape. Spoon into the buns.

3. Halve the passion fruit and scoop the pulp and juice into a bowl. Gradually add the remaining confectioners' sugar, beating until the mixture thickly coats the back of the spoon. If the passion fruit are very juicy, you may need extra sugar. Spoon over the buns so the frosting runs down the sides.

PLUM TRIPITI

MAKES 24
- 3½ oz feta cheese, drained and coarsely shredded
- Heaping ⅓ cup ricotta cheese
- ¼ cup superfine sugar
- ¼ teaspoon ground cinnamon
- 1 large egg, lightly beaten
- ⅓ cup (½ stick plus 1⅓ tablespoons) unsalted butter
- 12 sheets of phyllo dough, thawed if frozen but chilled
- All-purpose flour, for dusting
- 1 lb small red plums, halved and pitted
- Sifted confectioners' sugar, for dusting

1. Preheat the oven to 400°F. In a bowl, mix together the feta, ricotta, sugar, cinnamon, and egg. In a small saucepan, melt the butter.

2. Working quickly, lay one sheet of phyllo dough on a work surface, with the short edge toward you. (Keep the remaining sheets of phyllo dough covered with a clean dish towel to prevent drying out.) Brush the phyllo with a bit of the melted butter, then cut in half to make two long strips. Place a spoonful of the cheese mixture a short way up from the bottom left-hand corner of each strip, then cover with a plum half. Fold the bottom right-hand corner of one strip diagonally over the plum to cover the filling and to make a triangle. Fold the bottom left-hand corner upward to make a second triangle, then keep folding until the top of the strip is reached and the filling is enclosed in a triangle of phyllo. Place on a cookie sheet and repeat until 24 triangles have been made, using all the filling.

3. Brush the outside of the triangles with the remaining butter and bake in the oven for about 10 minutes, until the phyllo is golden and the plum juices begin to run from the sides. Dust with sifted confectioners' sugar and let cool for 15 minutes before serving.

SWEET POTATO MERINGUE PIE

SERVES 6

- Butter, for greasing
- Single quantity Pâte Sucrée (see page 16), chilled
- All-purpose flour, for dusting
- 1 lb sweet potato, peeled and diced
- ⅔ cup heavy cream
- Heaping ⅓ light brown sugar
- 2 tablespoons clear honey
- 1 teaspoon ground ginger

- 1 teaspoon pumpkin pie spie
- 1 large egg
- 3 large egg yolks

Meringue topping
- 3 large egg whites
- ¼ cup light brown sugar
- ¼ cup superfine sugar
- ½ teaspoon ground ginger

1. Grease an 8-inch metal piece dish 2 inches deep. Roll out the pastry on a lightly floured work surface and use to line the pie dish, then chill for 15 minutes. Preheat the oven to 350°F.

2. Put the sweet potato in the top of a steamer, cover, and cook until tender, about 10 minutes. Mash with the cream, sugar, honey, and spices, then beat in the whole egg and egg yolks. Pour into the pie shell, level the surface, and bake in the oven for 40 minutes, until set.

3. Make the topping. In a clean, dry, grease-free bowl, whip the egg whites until they form stiff peaks, then gradually beat in the sugars, a teaspoonful at a time. Add the ginger and whip until very thick and glossy, another 1–2 minutes. Spoon over the hot pie and swirl the meringue with the back of a spoon. Bake for 15 minutes, until lightly browned and the meringue is crisp. Let cool for 30 minutes, then cut into wedges and serve warm with scoops of vanilla ice cream.

TIP

- For spiced pumpkin meringue pie, use 1 lb seeded pumpkin in place of the sweet potato. Peel, dice, and steam as above, then mash with the cream, spices, and egg yolks and bake in the pie shell. Top with the meringue and bake as above.

APRICOT & PISTACHIO PURSES

- -

MAKES 8
- ⅓ cup (½ stick plus 1⅓ tablespoons) butter, softened
- 2 tablespoons superfine sugar
- Few drops of almond extract or orange flower water
- 1 medium egg yolk
- ¼ cup ground almonds
- ¼ cup coarsely chopped pistachios
- 8 apricots
- 4 sheets of phyllo dough, 19 inches x 9 inches, thawed if frozen but chilled
- Sifted confectioners' sugar, for dusting

1. In a bowl, beat 2 tablespoons (¼ stick) of the butter with the superfine sugar and almond extract or orange flower water until pale and smooth. Add the egg yolk and ground almonds and mix well, then stir in the pistachios. Chill for 15 minutes.

2. Preheat the oven to 375°F. Cut each apricot in half, discard the pits, then sandwich the apricots back together with the pistachio mixture.

3. In a saucepan, melt the remaining butter. Working quickly, lay one sheet of phyllo dough on a work surface. (Keep the remaining sheets of phyllo dough covered with a clean dish towel to prevent drying out.) Brush the phyllo with a bit of the melted butter, then cut into four rectangles. Place an apricot on one of the rectangles, lift up the corners of the phyllo to enclose the apricot, then pinch together at the top of the fruit. Wrap a second phyllo rectangle at right angles to the first to form a purse shape. Repeat with a second apricot and two more phyllo rectangles, then place on a cookie sheet. Repeat with the remaining apricots.

4. Brush the purses with the remaining butter, then bake in the oven for 15 minutes, until golden. Dust with sifted confectioners' sugar and serve warm or cold with scoops of vanilla ice cream.

INDEX

GLOSSARY

- All-purpose flour = plain flour
- Allspice, apple pie mix = mixed spice
- Baking soda = bicarbonate of soda
- Celery root = celeriac
- Cilantro = coriander
- Confectioners' sugar = icing sugar
- Cornstarch = cornflour
- Corn syrup = golden syrup
- Dark corn syrup = treacle
- Decorating tip = nozzle
- Dill weed = dill
- Eggplant = aubergine
- Golden raisins = sultanas
- Jelly = jam
- Jellyroll pan = Swiss roll tin
- Light brown sugar = muscovado sugar
- Light cream = single cream
- Phyllo pastry = filo pastry
- Pie shell = pie case
- Plastic wrap = clingfilm
- Preserved ginger = stem ginger
- Pumpkin pie spice = mixed spice
- Scallions = spring onions
- Semisweet chocolate = plain chocolate
- Superfine sugar = caster sugar
- Tomato paste = tomato purée

PICTURE CREDITS